Teaching the Five Themes of Geography

written by Bonnie Dill
illustrated by Leah Raechel Killeen

FS-10148 Teaching the Five Themes of Geography
All rights reserved–Printed in the U.S.A.
Copyright © 1994 Frank Schaffer Publications, Inc.
23740 Hawthorne Blvd.
Torrance, CA 90505

Table of Contents

INTRODUCTION

This book provides teachers many ideas, within a structured approach, of how to teach geography. It focuses on the five themes of geography—**location, place, human-environment interaction, movement, and regions.** These themes were articulated by the Joint Committee on Geographic Education of the National Council for Geographic Education and the Association of American Geographers. The publication that introduces these themes is entitled "Guidelines for Geographic Education." This committee formed in response to the concern that geography education was at risk in America. Put simply, geography was a nebulous area of study because, beyond the question "Where is it?" there were no guidelines for teaching about places.

Teachers, like yourself, are concerned about giving students a perspective that will avoid a stereotypical view of the world's people and places. Geography seems and is the appropriate subject toward this end, but without a structure, it has been difficult to proceed. That is why the recognition of geography as a study revolving around five distinct themes is so exciting. No longer can we ignore geography as a valid subject for education and schools.

A solid knowledge of geography will provide students with an invaluable tool for their lives. They will use it to choose a place to live, to vacation, and to work. As voters, they will use it to make choices about the future of our earth. Without a geographically educated population, the democratic process of our country will not serve the better interests of our towns, states, nation, and world. It is increasingly obvious that our actions here in the United States of America have profound effects on the rest of the world. The impact of foreign decisions is in turn felt by us. We must give our students the working knowledge necessary to compete and cooperate in a global society.

Herein lies a seed of opportunity for teachers in their quest for inspiring students to be the best they can be. The quality of our lives and those of generations to come depends on geographic sensitivity. Using the five themes of geography, teachers can provide students with a perspective of the world in its parts or as a whole. One place, studied with the five themes, becomes alive in a student's mind. The relationship of that one place to any other one place becomes clear when using this approach. Teachers and students cannot help but be excited by the way that the five themes of geography include them personally in the fabric of the world.

CHAPTER ONE

LOCATION

The theme of "location" is the basis of geographic education. It asks the question "Where is it?" Every day we are faced with opportunities to answer such a question silently to ourselves and sometimes as a response to someone's question. As we watch the news or read the newspaper, we organize the information we hear in many ways. One category always exists—location. **Everything happens somewhere.**

Still we ask, though, "Where is that, anyway?" And the response can take two forms—**Relative** or **Absolute Location.**

Here is an example of how one could answer a "location" question:

Where is Manila? Answer: It is at 15°N, 121°E.

Yes, that is where Manila is and always will be, absolutely. Giving the longitude and latitude of a place is the *absolute location*.

This type of response is not a conversational answer, however. More often the response relates the place to another place, as in the following:

Question: Where is Manila? Answers: In the northern part of the Philippines. South of Japan. Near Vietnam.

These answers are examples of *relative location*.

Even though Manila is southwest of Tokyo, it is in the Northern and Eastern Hemispheres.

Relative and absolute location combined can be very confusing for the middle school student. The activities in this chapter are designed to practice the skills of absolute and relative location.

The Human Grid

Objective: Students will gain an understanding of the abstract concepts of relative and absolute location using the directions of north, south, east, and west, along with longitude and latitude.

Preparation: To study a place, one needs to know *where* it is. Ask students the question "Where is (your hometown)?"

Use the concept of **near** to start this activity. Ask what direction on a map they would travel to get from the neighboring town to their town. Then ask the question as if they were traveling from a different neighboring town to their town. Establish that the location of a place is relative to where you are coming from.

Place the desks, or students sitting on the floor, in rows, forming a grid.

Procedure:

Part I

Assume that if you faced the front of your classroom you would be facing north; the back, south; the right, east; the left, west. Share this with the students. Ask one student where another student is seated in relation to him or her. For example, if the student would have to move forward three seats and to the left one seat, he/she would have to travel northwest to get to the other student. Make up a few examples and then let students make up examples for one another.

Part II

Designate the very middle person in your room as coordinate 0°,0°. The whole column, then, running north to south, is 0°E/W. And the whole row, running east to west is 0°N/S. The next column to the left (if you face the back of the room) is designated as 10° E. The column to the right of 0° is 10° W. Move in tens until all rows and columns are labeled. To make the concept more concrete, place a sheet of paper on the floor at the end of each row and column with the appropriate designation on it.

Now you have created a grid of people. Make up 3" x 5" cards with all the possible coordinates in the classroom, placing one on each card. An example grid with 25 students is shown below.

front of classroom				
20°N, 20°W	20°N, 10°W	20°N, 0°E/W	20°N, 10°E	20°N, 20°E
10°N, 20°W	10°N, 10°W	10°N, 0°E/W	10°N, 10°E	10°N, 20°E
0°N/S, 20°W	0°N/S, 10°W	0°N/S, 0°E/W	0°N/S, 10°E	0°N/S, 20°E
10°S, 20°W	10°S, 10°W	10°S, 0°E/W	10°S, 10°E	10°S, 20°E
20°S, 20°W	20°S, 10°W	20°S, 0°E/W	20°S, 10°E	20°S, 20°E
back of classroom				

Lay the coordinate cards on a table. Have students then come up and select the card with coordinates they think identifies where they are sitting. Tell them to keep it face down so others cannot see the card they selected. (If you have one student who would be willing to select the wrong one on purpose, coach him/her to do so.)

Randomly choose a student. Call on another student to say aloud what coordinate he or she thinks that student should have selected. Have that student reveal his/her answer. If they agree, confirm the answer. Eventually, you will have someone voice a coordinate that does not agree with the one a student selected (especially if you set it up to happen). See how many agree with each student and then reveal the correct answer.

Give each student a chance to guess someone else's coordinates.

As a challenge, change the coordinates so that they move by 20° for each row or move the origin. Have students figure out the new coordinates in their heads.

Other Ideas: As students enter the room the next day, give each a coordinate card and have them find their seats for the day's activity. You can also assign seats if you need or want a certain seating arrangement for the next activity.

Jenny is at 20°N, 10°E!

That Is Absolutely Right!

Objective: Students will be able to locate places in an atlas by using longitude and latitude coordinates.

Preparation: This activity is used after students have had some practice with longitude and latitude and hemispheres.

Copy the two lists of places with their latitude and longitude coordinates from the next page. Make enough copies so that half the class will have List A and half, List B.

Procedure: Divide students into pairs. Give one person List A and the other List B. Tell them not to let their partners see their lists. Give each student, or partner, an atlas. Partner A then says, "What city is at 43°N, 71°W?" (or whatever the first example is on their list). Partner B looks in the atlas at those coordinates and says, "Portland, Maine." Partner A corroborates the answer. Then Partner B gives Partner A a question. They switch back and forth until they use all the examples on their list. Then allow students to make up some of their own for one another. Students think this is fun because, of course, they try to choose the most obscure places.

Monitor students when they do this to make certain they are steering one another correctly.

That Is Absolutely Right!
List A

Give your partner the coordinates of the city. The partner finds those coordinates and guesses the city. Hide the answers from your partner.

1. 41 °N, 29°E
   Istanbul, Turkey

2. 51°N, 4°E
   Brussels, Belgium

3. 37°N, 3°E
   Algiers, Algeria

4. 30°N, 31°E
   Cairo, Egypt

5. 14°N, 100°E
   Bangkok, Thailand

6. 15°N, 121°E
   Manila, Philippines

7. 32°S, 116°E
   Perth, Australia

8. 16°N, 33°E
   Khartoum, Sudan

9. 47°N, 71°W
   Quebec City, Quebec

10. 30°N, 95°W
    Houston, Texas

That Is Absolutely Right
List B

Give your partner the coordinates of the city. The partner finds those coordinates and guesses the city. Hide the answers from your partner.

1. 56°N, 38°E
   Moscow, Russia

2. 40°N, 4°W
   Madrid, Spain

3. 59°N, 18°E
   Stockholm, Sweden

4. 50°N, 19°E
   Katowice, Poland

5. 6°S, 107°E
   Jakarta, Indonesia

6. 41°S, 175°E
   Wellington, New Zealand

7. 15°N, 17°W
   Dakar, Senegal

8. 34°N, 8°W
   Casablanca, Morocco

9. 48°N, 122°W
   Seattle, Washington

10. 43°N, 88°W
    Milwaukee, Wisconsin

Places, Everyone!

Objective: Students will practice finding places in an atlas using the absolute location skills associated with longitude and latitude.

Preparation: Copy and cut the descriptions of places on the next few pages. These descriptions tell some facts about famous places, structures, events, or land forms in the world. To make them last from year to year, consider mounting them on construction paper or index cards and laminating. Copy enough "Places, Everyone!" activity sheets for each student.

Procedure: Distribute to each student a place card, a "Places Everyone!" activity sheet, and an atlas. They must determine in what city or area of the world this place is and find it in the atlas. Next, they write down the absolute location or longitude and latitude.

To find some of the locations will take research. Have a classroom set of encyclopedias available or take the class to the library. This is an excellent opportunity to develop appropriate work for the heterogeneous classroom. Be purposeful in giving difficult examples to those with higher skills and easier ones to those with lower-level skills. If you prefer to bypass the research piece of this activity, give students the answers that complete the blanks on the place cards. These answers reveal where the event, structure, or land form occurs. There is an answer sheet provided.

When each student has found his/her place and the correct longitude and latitude, gather the class back together.

Have a student stand and read what is on his/her place card, leaving the answer that completes the blank undisclosed. He or she then reveals the coordinates of the place. The rest of the class find the coordinates in their atlases and raise their hands when they think they have the answer that correctly completes the blank. The student whose turn it is calls on someone to say the answer and confirms whether the answer is correct.

Give each student a chance to do his/her example. Surprise! They are learning some cultural literacy at the same time.

The Eiffel Tower

In 1889, the Eiffel Tower was constructed as an example of the usefulness of iron as a building material. It was the most impressive display at the World's Fair that year. Over three hundred meters high, the tower weighs seven metric tons. Its base covers two and one-half acres. Visitors are amazed at this incredible piece of workmanship when they visit the famous city of _____.

The Sphinx

Carved out of rock to resemble King Khafre, a pharaoh of 4,500 years ago, the Sphinx rises 66 feet above the desert. In the past, soldiers used its nose for target practice when shooting guns, so much of the face is destroyed. With the head of a person and the body of a lion, this ominous statue gains much attention when tourists visit _____.

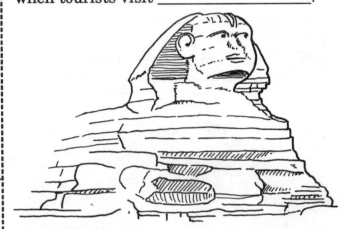

Mount Fuji

This now-dormant volcano last erupted in 1707. Considered sacred by the local people, there is a pilgrimage to this mountain each year; over 60,000 people hike to the summit. The snow-capped peak rises 12,388 feet above sea level on the island country of

_____.

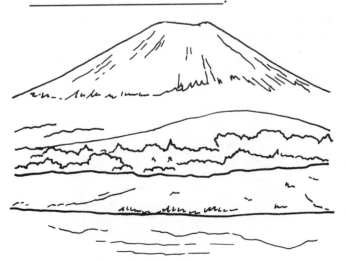

Yellowstone National Park

In search of beaver pelts, fur traders from Europe were the first to explore the area now known as Yellowstone. In 1872, it became the first national park in the United States. A famous geyser, Old Faithful, erupts in the park every 33 to 96 minutes. Because of the wide variety of wildlife that live in the park's boundaries, signs such as "Don't feed the bears" are a common sight when visiting Yellowstone. Its borders reach three states: _____, _____, and _____.

Chichen Itza

The famous ruins of a Mayan city, Chichen Itza contains an example of the well-known ball courts used by these early Americans. The Great Ball Court is an incredible 270 feet in length. The largest pyramid in the city is called El Castillo. Probably built in the sixth century, Chichen Itza was mysteriously abandoned after a thousand years of inhabitance. The thick growth of the jungles covered this amazing city for centuries until it was later discovered on the _____ Peninsula.

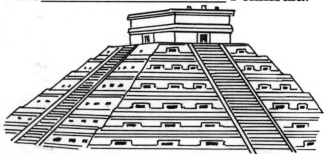

Great Wall of China

To protect against invaders, the Great Wall of China was built over 2,000 years ago. Most likely the largest construction project ever undertaken, the Wall stretches for 1,500 miles. People worked for lifetimes on the Wall, and it is rumored that when they died on the job, their bodies were built into the section under construction. The top of the Wall made a smooth road-like surface for messengers to travel on, too. So, the Wall served as a great asset in times of war, for protection and communication, until the airplane was invented. The Wall starts near the Bo Hai coast, an inlet of the _____ Sea.

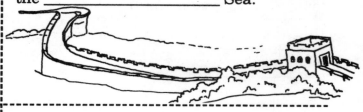

Machu Picchu

Once the great city of the Incas, Machu Picchu remains today as an incredible example of early American settlement. The city was built of huge, precisely cut stone blocks that were somehow carried up the mountainside without the use of the wheel. More than 3,000 steps serve to connect the terraced gardens and irrigation systems, methods still used today by the people of mountainous nations. In 1911 this "lost city" was rediscovered high in the Andes in the country of _____.

Colosseum

In the days of gladiators, young boys went to special schools to learn how to fight with lions and other fierce animals. They would then perform their acquired skills, most often to the death, in front of great crowds at the Colosseum. This huge amphitheater sat up to 50,000 people on marble benches. Many forms of entertainment happened there, the most famous being the gladiator events. Everyone eagerly went to these bloody games located in the city of _____.

Statue of Liberty

Liberty Enlightening the World, her original name, was dedicated by President Cleveland in 1886. The Statue of Liberty is a symbol of friendship between France and the United States, built by the French sculptor Bartholdi. The stone tablet in her left hand is dated July 4, 1776, as a reminder of Independence Day. Standing over 160 feet high and weighing 225 tons, the lady in the harbor of the city of

_____ is a big monument to freedom and hope.

Grand Canyon

An awesome display of the power of erosion can be seen when you visit the Grand Canyon. Thousands of years of wind and water travel have carved out the beautiful sight of layer upon layer of colored rock. People hike down the canyon on foot and by mule to explore the canyon's depths and perhaps raft the mighty Colorado River that flows swiftly through the wilderness below. The town named after the national park, Grand Canyon, lies within its perimeter in the state of _____.

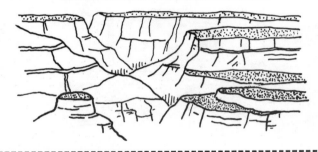

Stonehenge

The great mystery of why Stonehenge was built has been tossed around for centuries. No one is certain of its significance, but experts believe it was used as a solar calendar between 2000 and 1400 B.C. Each stone is almost 30 feet long and weighs up to 50 tons. Recently, a barricade has been put up to keep visitors from climbing on the rocks and wearing them away. The curious arrangement of stones is located in the country of _____.

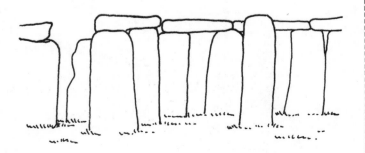

Leaning Tower of Pisa

Originally planned as a bell tower to be completed quickly and easily by craftsmen of the day, the Tower of Pisa ended up taking 700 years to construct. The soil underneath the Tower is not of the quality to support such a heavy structure of white marble. Engineers have tried to design reinforcements to straighten the Tower, but it continues to lean so severely that people in the town of Pisa place bets on when it will topple. Pisa is in the country of _____.

Taj Mahal

From 1632 to 1654, over 20,000 workers labored to complete the Taj Mahal. The tomb of Mumtaz-Mahal, wife of emperor Shah Jahan, is considered the most beautiful mausoleum in the world. The Taj Mahal is crafted with millions of tiles in mosaic designs and is surrounded by immaculate gardens and waterways for tourists to enjoy. It is located in the country of _____.

Mount Everest

The Sherpa, Himalayan mountain people, claim to have spotted and tracked the Yeti, known to Americans as the Abominable Snowman. But treks to the summit of Everest, the tallest mountain on earth, have claimed many lives due to severe weather conditions, not due to the rage of a creature unscientifically documented. The people close to Everest call her the "Goddess Mother of the World." Scientists are estimating, though, that erosion will rob Everest of its claim to fame in the near future as K2, another mountain in the Himalayan range, achieves "tallest mountain" status. Everest borders the countries of _____ and _____.

Suez Canal

In 1869, ships could finally avoid the dangerous trips around the Cape of Good Hope in Africa. After nearly 10 years of digging through the land in the Sinai Peninsula, a waterway was opened and world trade began to flourish. Being 40 feet deep and 179 feet wide, even the world's largest ships can pass through, shortening their journeys considerably. Called the Suez Canal it allows ships to pass from the _____ Sea to the _____ Sea.

Wailing Wall

An ancient temple of great religious significance stood here in biblical times. With the invasion of the Romans in A.D. 70, all but a portion of the western wall was destroyed. The Jewish still gather to pray in the spirit of the temple that once stood in the city of _____.

Victoria Falls

Located in Africa on the _____ River, Victoria Falls is about one and one-half times as wide and twice as high as Niagara Falls. The great tons of water that flow over the falls send up a mist that can, at times, be seen from 37 miles away. The spray creates a huge cloud over the falls that reaches over 1,000 feet high. A great roaring sound can be heard from miles away, hence the local name of the Falls is Mosi-oa-tunya—Smoke that Thunders.

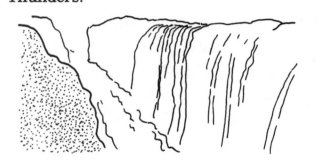

Angel Falls

Atop Devil's Mountain is Angel Falls, the highest waterfall in the world, at 2,646 feet. The falls were named after a pilot, James Angel. He was flying over the dense jungles in the country of _____ in search of a lost river deposit of gold nuggets he had once seen from another plane. In 1935 he spotted the falls and reported them. In 1937 he tried to land his plane on top of the mountain to reach the falls on foot but was unsuccessful due to the harsh environment of the forest. In 1949, his claim to have discovered the highest waterfall was proven by an American-lead expedition.

Tower of London

The Tower of London stands as a symbol of royal history in England. It has been an ornately decorated palace for the royalty, a prison with torture chambers and famous executions, a fortress, and a museum. In the true sense of medieval castles, the Tower of London was once surrounded by a moat. It lies on the north bank of the River _____, once overlooking the old walled City of London. Executed there were two wives of King Henry VIII, the Little Princess, and numerous others. Today the museum in the Tower holds the world-famous Crown Jewels.

The Parthenon

The Parthenon is an ancient Greek temple which sits atop the _____ high above _____. It is a fine example of Greek architecture designed to honor Athena, the Greek goddess.
The Parthenon underwent an explosion in 1687 and was mostly destroyed. Today, only a shell remains.

Name _____

Places Everyone!

Look at the list on these sheets and find the famous place that is on your card. They are listed here in alphabetical order. Fill in the appropriate information about your place.

Later, as other students in the class report the absolute location of each place, fill in the correct information below.

Angel Falls is in the country of _____.

        absolute location: _____, _____

Chichen Itza is on the _____ Peninsula.

        absolute location: _____, _____

The **Colosseum** is in the city of _____.

        absolute location: _____, _____

The **Eiffel Tower** is in the city of _____.

        absolute location: _____, _____

The **Grand Canyon** is in the state of _____.

        absolute location:
        begins at   _____, _____

        ends at   _____, _____

The **Great Wall of China** starts on the Bo Hai coast, an inlet of the _____ Sea.

        absolute location:
        begins at   _____, _____

        ends at   _____, _____

Name _____

Places Everyone!

The **Leaning Tower of Pisa** is in the country of _____.

absolute location: _____, _____

Machu Picchu is in the country of _____.

absolute location: _____, _____

Mount Everest borders the countries of _____ and _____.

absolute location: _____, _____

Mount Fuji is on the island country of _____.

absolute location: _____, _____

The **Parthenon** is in the city of _____.

absolute location: _____, _____

The **Sphinx** is in the city of _____.

absolute location: _____, _____

The **Statue of Liberty** is in _____ harbor.

absolute location: _____, _____

Stonehenge is located in the country of _____.

absolute location: _____, _____

Places Everyone!

The **Suez Canal** connects the _____ Sea to the _____ Sea .

absolute location:
begins at _____ _____, _____
ends at _____, _____

The **Taj Mahal** is in the country of _____.

absolute location: _____, _____

The **Tower of London** is on the River _____.

absolute location: _____, _____

Victoria Falls is in Africa on the _____ River.

absolute location: _____, _____

The **Wailing Wall** is in the city of _____.

absolute location: _____, _____

Yellowstone National Park's borders reach the three states of _____,
_____, and _____.

absolute location: _____, _____

absolute location of Old Faithful geyser close to the
center of the park _____, _____

Each "Places Everyone!" activity card has a blank for students to complete. Students also are responsible for identifying the absolute location of the places assigned.

Below is a list of the famous places found on the activity cards with the **answers** for the blanks and the *approximate* longitude and latitude coordinates.

Angel Falls
absolute location:

". . . in the country of **Venezuela**."
6°N,63°W

Chichen Itza
absolute location:

". . . later discovered in the **Yucatan** Peninsula."
21°N,88°W

Colosseum
absolute location:

". . . in the city of **Rome**."
42°N,13°E

Eiffel Tower
absolute location:

". . . the famous city of **Paris**."
49°N,2°E

Grand Canyon
absolute location:

". . .in the state of **Arizona**."
37°N,113°E

Great Wall of China
absolute location:

". . . starts on the Bo Hai coast, an inlet of the **Yellow Sea**."
40°N,120°E to 39°N,100°E

Leaning Tower of Pisa
absolute location:

". . . in the country of **Italy**."
44°N,10°E

Machu Picchu
absolute location:

". . . the Andes in the country of **Peru**."
13°S,72°W

Mount Everest
absolute location:

". . . borders the countries of **Nepal** and **China**."
28°N,87°E

Mount Fuji
absolute location:

". . . the island country of **Japan**."
36°N,138°E

Parthenon
absolute location:

". . . in the city of **Athens**."
38°N,24°E

Sphinx
absolute location:

". . . when tourists visit **Giza**."
30°N,31°E

Statue of Liberty absolute location:	". . . the lady in **New York** harbor." 41°N,74°W
Stonehenge absolute location:	". . . is located in the country of **Great Britain (England)**" 51°N,2°W
Suez Canal absolute location:	". . . from the **Mediterannean** Sea to the **Red** Sea." 30°N,33°E
Taj Mahal absolute location:	". . . is the country of **India's** pride and joy." 27°N,78°E
Tower of London absolute location:	". . . of the River **Thames**." 51°N,0°W
Victoria Falls absolute location:	". . . in Africa on the **Zambezi** River." 18°S,26°E
Wailing Wall absolute location:	". . . the town of **Jerusalem**." 32°N,35°E
Yellowstone National Park absolute location:	". . . Its borders reach three states, **Wyoming, Montana,** and **Idaho**." 45°N,111°W

 FS-10148 Teaching the Five Themes of Geography

CHAPTER TWO

PLACE

Every place on earth has its own special qualities that make it different from other places. To gain a wholistic perspective of a place one has to consider two general things—**physical** and **human characteristics**.

Physical characteristics are things determined by nature, such as climate, land forms, indigenous plants and animals, and types of soil.

Human characteristics can be defined by the culture of a place in, for example, the language, clothing, architectural styles, and governmental ideologies. The routes of transportation, communication networks, and the choices people make for business and livelihood also influence the character of a place.

To describe a place with just physical characteristics does not give a person a complete understanding of the place. One must include the human aspects as well. For example, a travel brochure describing a place with many beaches, a warm climate, and semi-tropical vegetation may sound alluring. Your mind may take you on a trip to the Florida Keys. You could, however, be on your way to Cuba, a place with physical characteristics similar to Florida. Not mentioning the human characteristics of a Communist government, Spanish-speaking people, and a different standard of living would be deceiving to the person reading the brochure.

Similarly, an English-speaking, interstate-accessible, well-planned city could be Denver, Colorado, or Atlanta, Georgia. With similar human characteristics, the two places are still very different because of their physical surroundings.

Place is a theme of geography that conjures up a mental picture of a place with people going about their everyday lives in their familiar environment. Place is the personality of geography.

Why Is This Place Famous?

We have all heard of places like the Taj Mahal and the Grand Canyon. The first time hearing of a famous place, do you remember thinking, "Why is this place famous?"

Objective: Students will learn about famous places in the world as a step toward cultural literacy. They will determine if the places are famous due to their physical or human characteristics. They will locate the places using absolute and relative location skills.

Preparation: Copy and distribute to each student the "Why Is This Place Famous?" activity sheet.

Procedure: Have each student select a place that he or she would like to research. A list of possible places is included entitled "Famous Places to Research." Some students may show particular interest in one place or another while others will be satisfied with a randomly assigned place. Either have the materials available for them in the classroom or take them to the library to do the research.

Each student must create a poster of his/her place which includes:

- a drawing of the place (or part of the place)
- a paragraph, in his/her own words, that describes the place
- a map showing where in the world the place is, including the longitude and latitude

Have each student share the poster when he/she is done so that the whole class learns about a variety of famous places and why they are famous.

An example is sketched in miniature here:

Other Ideas: Have real photos, slides, or pictures from books available to show the whole class as students present their posters. Or after the presentations, show the real pictures and have students try to identify the famous places about which they have just heard.

Give students a world map on which to write the locations of famous places as their classmates present them.

Have slides or transparencies of all the famous places available for students to use as a tracing guide for their posters. The drawings are then very realistic and more identifiable.

Copy a world map of your choice or the one in the back of the book and have students glue it to their poster rather than draw their own. Have each student develop an icon (a small representational drawing) for the famous place. Use the icon to mark the location of the famous place on the map.

Invite parents into the classroom to help with the research, writing process, and poster design. To give students a different kind of audience experience, ask parents to come for the presentations. You may want parents and/or students to help with the evaluation portion of this activity if appropriate to your classroom style.

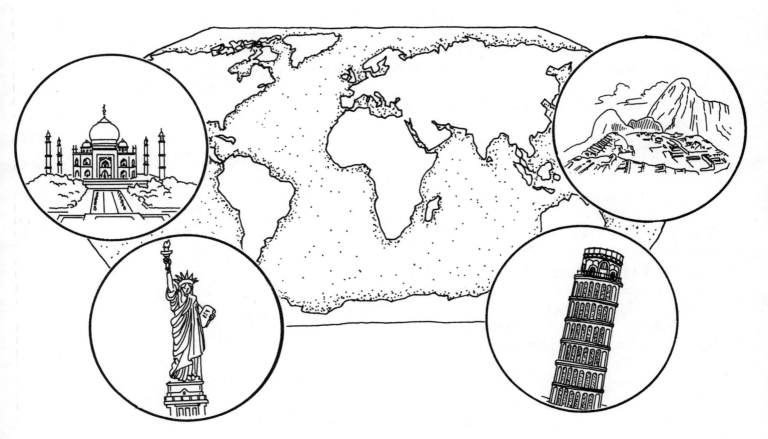

Famous Places to Research

Versailles
The Forbidden City
Yosemite
The White House
Victoria Falls
Ming Tombs
Borobudur
Vatican
Sydney Opera House
Acropolis
Kilimanjaro
Golden Gate Bridge
Shwe Dagon Pagoda
Yellowstone
Tower of London
Easter Island
Petra
Great Wall of China
Tikal
Dead Sea
Big Ben
Mauna Loa
Bourbon Street
Wailing Wall
Terra Cotta Warriors of Xi`an

Mt. Everest
Stonehenge
Monument Valley
Central Park
Arc de Triomphe
Ayer's Rock
St. Paul's Cathedral
Sugarloaf Mountain
Great Barrier Reef
Mt. McKinley
Dracula's Castle
Taj Mahal
Crater Lake
Buckingham Palace
Aswan Dam
Sphinx
Seattle Space Needle
Kremlin
Mt. St. Helens
Leaning Tower of Pisa
Petrified Forest
Pompeii
Empire State Building
Mt. Pinatubo

Windsor Castle
Disney World
Niagara Falls
Carlsbad Caverns
Matterhorn
Mt. Rushmore
St. Louis Arch
Statue of Liberty
Westminster Abbey
Machu Picchu
Great Zimbabwe Ruins
Biosphere II
Eiffel Tower
Lochness Lake
Grand Canyon
Panama Canal
Baalbek
Chichen Itza
Louvre
K2
Angel Falls
Colosseum
Dome of the Rock
Bermuda Triangle
Alamo

Seven Wonders of Antiquity:

The Olympian Zeus
The Pharaohs at Alexandria
The Hanging Gardens of Babylon
The Colossus of Rhodes
The Pyramids of Giza
The Temple of Artemis at Ephesus
The Mausoleum at Halicarnassus

Why Is This Place Famous?

The name of my famous place is _____.

It is located in _____.

The absolute location, longitude and latitude, of my place is _____.

Relative to my hometown, the direction I would have to travel to go to my famous place is: (circle one)

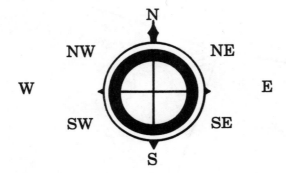

My place is famous for its (human, physical) characteristics.

Here is a brief description of my famous place:

_____

_____

_____

_____

_____

_____

The book(s) where I found my information are listed here with relevant page numbers for future reference.

_____

_____

_____

Geography Terms Booklet

Objective: Students will use the definitions of common land forms to identify real examples of land forms on maps.

Students create a 10-page geography-terms booklet using real-world land forms as examples for each term. The assignment sheet on the following page details all requirements for the booklet.

Shown below are illustrations of the two possible layout styles that students can use.

Preparation: Make two poster-size sample pages, similar to the examples on the previous page, to show to students as the directions are given.

Materials: markers, crayons, colored pencils, pencils, erasers, atlases, encyclopedias

Per student:
- 10 half sheets of white construction paper
- 2 colored half sheets of construction paper for cover pages
- geography word list (attached)
- assignment sheet (attached)

Procedure: Distribute the "Geography Terms Booklet" and the "Geography Terms List" to each student. Read the directions aloud. Use the posters as graphic organizers to show how the five criteria for each page have been met. Encourage students to use the checklist for each booklet page they produce.

For younger students, demonstrate how the information for the sample pages was found.

For example: The samples given show the word *swamp*. Look up *swamp* in an encyclopedia as the class observes. Read the entry to students. Usually encyclopedias have real-world examples of the land form words.

World Book, for instance, gives the definition of swamp and then lists the Okefenokee, the Everglades, and the Dismal Swamp.

Demonstrate how to find one of the real-world examples in an atlas. Some index listings have common abbreviations for land forms that students can learn to look for and use. Symbols used on the keys of some maps are also helpful.

A listing of examples is included for teacher reference.

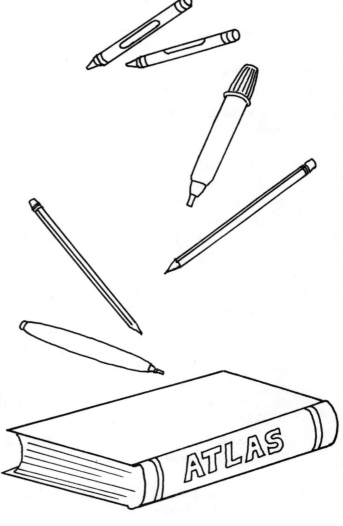

Evaluation: The student assignment sheet explains how the booklet is graded. It is the author's experience that the booklets are of higher quality when points are given for neatness and color. Therefore, each criterion is worth two points—one point for the item being present, and one point for neat and colorful work.

Teachers should feel free to make adaptations as necessary to the grading procedure and/or the assignment sheet itself.

Other Ideas: Pair students up. Each partner selects 10 different words to research and incorporate into the booklet. Between them, partners will have 20 examples to share with each other.

Choose some of the best booklets to display at your local library or bank. People love to look at them while waiting in line! This gives students a real audience for their work.

Further Evaluation: Since students have worked with only 10 of the 25 words available, the teacher may want to test students on all the terms and definitions. Below are ideas for reviewing the terms.

Reviewing:

1. Students make flashcards that have the word on one side and the definition on the other. Pairs make one set, then use it for quizzing each other.

   For teachers who see more than one period of social science students a day, have two periods make the cards and the others use them, too. With numerous sets of flashcards available, some may be taken home overnight as study aids. Save them to use each year during this activity.

2. Use the lesson entitled "Topo Quest" as a class review or as a test.

3. Offer incentive points on the test for doing extra pages in the booklet. For each extra page done by the student, he/she can earn a bonus point for the test. A perfect test score and a complete booklet would yield a 115 percent on the test. This could help a student's average at the end of the grading period.

4. Offer extra points on the test using the "Geography Terms Study Contract."

List A

archipelago–Indonesia, Canary Islands, Hawaiian Islands, West Indies
bay–Hudson, San Francisco, Bengal, Biscay
cape–Horn, of Good Hope, Canaveral, Cod
delta–Mississippi, Amazon, Nile
gulf–of Mexico, Persian, Carpentaria (Australia)
harbor–Boston, Hong Kong, Rio de Janeiro, Pearl
isthmus–Panama
oasis–many located in the Sahara and Arabian Deserts
strait–of Gibraltar, Bering, of Magellan, of Florida
tributary–The Missouri River is a tributary of the Mississippi River.

List B

canal–Erie, Panama, Suez
channel–English, Mozambique
desert–Sahara, Gobi, Mojave, Atacama
glacier–Glacier Bay in Alaska, Greenland, in the Alps, Himalayas
island–Barbados, Madagascar, Long Island, Vancouver
lake–Great Salt Lake, the Great Lakes, Titicaca, Victoria
mountain–Everest, McKinley, Kilimanjaro
mountain range–Himalayas, Andes, Alps, Rockies
mouth (of a river)–the opening of any river
peninsula–Florida, Sinai, Malay
plain–Great Plains, Pampas, West Siberian Plains
river–Nile, Amazon, Mississippi, Yangtze, Danube
swamp–Everglades, Okefenokee, Dismal
valley–Death, Ruhr, Loire
volcano–Mauna Loa, Mt. Saint Helens, Krakatoa, Pinatubo

Geography Terms Booklet

You will create a 10-page booklet of geography terms. Below is a checklist of the five items that will appear on each page.

Checklist

_____ 1. A geography term

_____ 2. The definition of the geography term

_____ 3. A drawing that shows what the definition means

_____ 4. A map section showing where one of these land forms exists

_____ 5. Use of the word in a sentence on the back of the page

---

Directions: Read both pages of this assignment sheet.

1. and 2. The Geography Terms and Definitions

Attached to this assignment are 25 geography terms and definitions. You must choose 10 terms from this list for your booklet. *Choose five terms from List A and five terms from List B.* On each page, you will write one term and its definition.

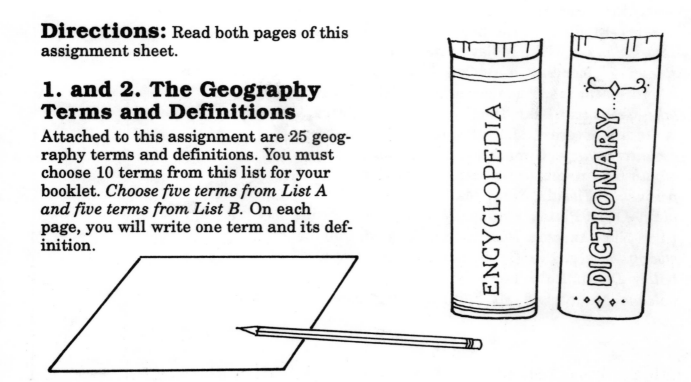

Geography Terms Booklet

3. and 4. The Drawings and the Map Sections

Using resources such as the encyclopedia, dictionary, and an atlas, research the term and find a real example of that land form somewhere in the world. Draw a map showing where the land form exists. You must label the surrounding features, countries, and states. The labeling is very important because it will identify *where* the landform is. Do not assume that the teacher will know of the place you have chosen.

You may use the map as the checklist no. 3 drawing if it appropriately shows the land form, as would drawing a *bay*. If, however, the map only shows the location of the land form, then a drawing is needed. For example, a map showing the location of a *desert* does not show what a desert looks like. For the term *desert* you might draw a sun shining on a sandy landscape with cactus growing.

5. Sentences

On the back of each page in your booklet, use the geography term found on that page in a sentence. This sentence will show that you understand the meaning of the word. General sentences in which any term could be inserted are not acceptable. For example, using the word *bay*:

Acceptable: We took the boat out for a ride in the bay.
Unacceptable: We went to the bay for a picnic. (You could go to the river, the mountain, or the desert for a picnic, too.)

Evaluation

You will be evaluated as follows. Each page has five items on it. Each item is worth two points. At 10 points per page, with a 10-page booklet, that adds up to 100 points.

This project will be graded not only on content but on the quality of your work. Therefore, the two points per item break down as follows:

    one point–for the item being present on the page

    one point–for neatness and color

Your Geography Terms Booklet is DUE on:

Name _____

Geography Terms List

List A

archipelago–a group of many islands

bay–part of an ocean or lake extending into the land and usually smaller than a gulf

cape–a point of land extending into a body of water

delta–a triangular deposit of sand and soil that collects at the mouth of some rivers

gulf–part of an ocean extending into land and usually larger than a bay

harbor–a sheltered area of water where ships can anchor safely

isthmus–a narrow strip of land with water on both sides, connecting two larger area of land

oasis–a fertile place in the desert where there is water and some vegetation

strait–a narrow waterway connecting two large bodies of water

tributary–a stream or river that flows into a larger stream or river

List B

canal–a waterway dug across land through which ships can pass through

channel–a narrow, deep waterway connecting two bodies of water; the deepest part of a river or waterway

desert–a dry, barren region that may be sandy and without trees

glacier–a huge mass of ice that moves slowly down a mountain

island–an area of land completely surrounded by water

lake–a large body of water surrounded by land

mountain–a land form with high elevation and a pointed or rounded top higher than a hill

mountain range–a row of connected mountains

mouth (of a river)–the part of a river where its waters flow into another body of water

peninsula–land surrounded by water on all sides but one

plain–a broad and flat or gently rolling area usually low in elevation

river–a large stream of water that flows into a lake, ocean, or other body of water

swamp–low, wet land that supports grass and trees

valley–low land between hills or mountains

volcano–an opening in the earth's surface through which steam, ashes, and lava are forced out

Name _____

Geography Terms Study Contract

The date of the Geography Terms Test is:

_____.

This contract is an agreement between two people:

the teacher and the student

The teacher agrees to give the student one extra point for each signature below. The student agrees to study at home for at least 15 minutes per day to acquire a signature. The student also agrees that all information and signatures below are valid.

_____   _____
Teacher's Signature   Student's Signature

Date _____ _____ Parent/Guardian Signature	Date _____ _____ Parent/Guardian Signature
Date _____ _____ Parent/Guardian Signature	Date _____ _____ Parent/Guardian Signature
Date _____ _____ Parent/Guardian Signature	Date _____ _____ Parent/Guardian Signature

Topo Quest

Objective: Students will identify physical features by applying geography terms to a fictitious map drawing.

Preparation: Copy student activity page" Topo Quest" onto an overhead transparency. Copy enough activity pages and "Topo Quest Word List" sheets for each student. Colored markers will be needed.

Note: "The Topo Quest Word List" uses the same words as are used in the activity called "Geography Terms Booklet." If definitions for these physical features are needed, refer to the "Geography Terms List."

Procedure: Distribute the student activity pages to each student. Allow students to work alone or in pairs. Set a time limit of 15 minutes. The object is to find as many land forms as possible on the "Topo Quest" drawing using the words on the "Topo Quest Word List." Instruct students to check off the words found.

Hang a large piece of plain chart paper, at least 30" x 36," on the wall. Project the "Topo Quest" transparency onto the paper.

When the time limit is up, students put their pencils down. Starting at the beginning of the "Topo Quest Word List" ask for a volunteer who found *archipelago*. The student uses the marker to write the word *archipelago* on the chart paper where the group of islands is projected. Confer with the class as to the correct placement of this word. Refer to the "Topo Quest Answer Key." Continue down the list, selecting students to fill in the drawing. There are instances where more than one answer can fit a certain land form. If a student can defend his or her answer it is correct.

As the activity proceeds, students may want to mark those they labeled correctly. The teacher can then ask who had the most items correctly identified.

Other Ideas: Include or eliminate Part II as described on the "Topo Quest Word List."

Some students may enjoy doing a "Topo Quest" drawing of their own.

Topo Quest Answer Key

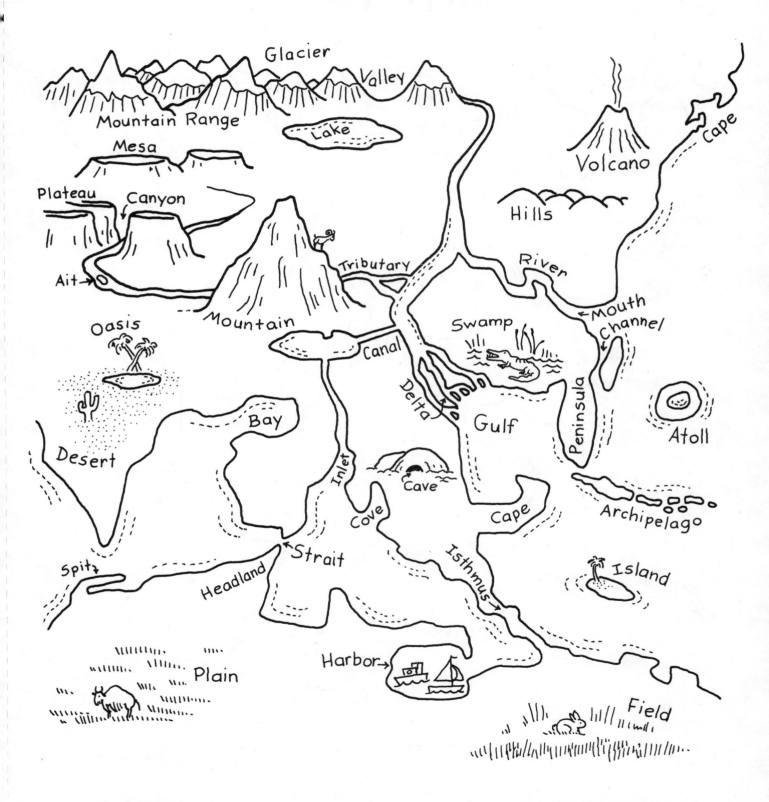

Glacier

Valley

Mountain Range

Mesa

Lake

Volcano

Cape

Plateau   Canyon

Hills

Ait

Tributary

River

Mouth

Channel

Mountain

Oasis

Swamp

Canal

Peninsula

Delta

Atoll

Desert

Bay

Gulf

Inlet

Cave

Cape

Archipelago

Cove

Spit

Strait

Isthmus

Island

Headland

Plain

Harbor

Field

Name _____

Topo Quest

Topo Quest Word List

Part I

Can you find these land forms on the "Topo Quest" drawing? Check them off as you find them. Label the drawing with the appropriate words.

_____	archipelago	_____	canal
_____	bay	_____	channel
_____	cape	_____	desert
_____	delta	_____	glacier
_____	gulf	_____	island
_____	harbor	_____	lake
_____	isthmus	_____	mountain
_____	oasis	_____	mountain range
_____	strait	_____	mouth
_____	tributary	_____	peninsula
_____	plain	_____	river
_____	swamp	_____	valley
_____	volcano	_____	field

Part II

Can you find other land forms that are not on this list? If so, list them here and label them on the drawing. Challenge a partner to find those that you discovered.

CHAPTER THREE

HUMAN - ENVIRONMENT INTERACTION

How do people affect the environment? How does the environment affect people? Looking at the effects that each has on the other is another important part of studying geography.

If you lived high in the Alps your house would look different from one in the Mid-East desert. In the Alps you would need a steeply pitched roof and plenty of insulation, neither of which would serve you well near the Persian Gulf. Physical surroundings are important determinants for life stlye.

The climate has much control over the crops that can be grown; therefore, the popular native foods are different everywhere. Corn dogs are a very common snack at fairs and malls in the midwestern United States. They are hot dogs covered with a cornbread dough, deep-fried on a stick. In the New England region of the United States it would be difficult to find a corn dog. Seeing that corn, a plains crop, sustains a good portion of the midwestern economy, it is not surprising where corn dogs are popular. Clothing styles, too, are associated with different regions. Why is silk used in traditional Japanese costumes?

Sometimes people are not satisfied with the resources of their natural environment and seek to change that environment for their own benefit. Damming rivers to make reservoirs, cutting forests to make room for housing projects, and creating landfills for garbage are examples of how people change the natural landscape. Preserving the habitat of endangered animals and town planning to reserve wooded areas for recreation are also ways that people interact with their environment. Some things that people do are positive and some are negative. The theme of **human-environment interaction** encourages people to study the impact that environmental changes will have on a place and the people who live there.

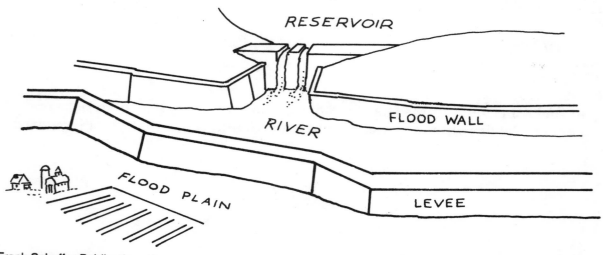

Photo Search Challenge

Objective: Students will identify ways in which the environment and human beings interact, affecting the life style choices people must make.

Preparation: This lesson has two parts the first time it is used in the classroom. Part I can be accomplished as a teacher preparation or as a student project (see options below–"Procedure"). After Part I has been completed once by the teacher or the students, the materials can be saved and used again with another class or during another year. The preparation of Part I is substantial; the reward is an easy-to-use, fun lesson for years to come.

A collection of photos from around the world is needed for this lesson. Gather *National Geographic* magazines and/or world travel magazines that may be cut. A plea to the community through the school newsletter or an inquiry at the public library can be helpful in accomplishing this task. Many people cannot bear to throw away their *National Geographics* but want to dispose of them to a worthy cause. Once the school library has a complete collection there is rarely a need for duplicates so this project, involving the cutting of photos from the magazines, is justified.

Materials: geographic/travel magazines, scissors, glue, construction paper

Procedure:

Part I

student project option

Divide students into five equal groups. With a focus on differing physical characteristics and climate, assign each group a country or region of the world. Five possibilities are Thailand, Switzerland, the MidEast, Kenya, and Iceland. Distribute the student activity sheet entitled, "_____ Photo Search." For each group, fill in the line with the name of the country or region they are researching. Ask students to complete the sheet and have it approved by the teacher.

Distribute magazines to groups according to the areas being researched. *National Geographic* has an external indexing system that makes this distribution task user friendly. Students skim through the magazines looking for photos that show some aspect of the physical characteristics or climate of their country/region. Ideally the photos should include human characteristics as well. For example, the rainforest of Thailand can be shown as the background in a photo of elephants being used as work animals to clear felled trees. Another example would be a photo of someone in the common MidEastern garb of a long white robe that protects from heat and sun. Before students cut the photos they should have the teacher approve their choice. Each student must find at least one photo and the group needs four or five photos altogether.

Idea: Photo possibilities to consider when cutting might include the following: crops, housing, clothing, animals, industries that relate to natural resources, recreation.

Students mount the photos onto individual pieces of construction paper and write the names of their countries/regions on the back. Once all the photos are gathered, the teacher shuffles the photos and randomly numbers them on the front. To facilitate Part II of the lesson, the teacher may choose to write a short clue on the front about what to focus on in the picture. Laminate the photos for lasting value.

Part I
teacher preparation option
The teacher may research the five country/region descriptions and search for appropriate photos instead of having students do it. As an example or for teacher use, there are five country/region descriptions provided on a following page. The photos to accompany these descriptions can be found in *National Geographic* with the help of an index in the library. Reference the countries and seek the appropriate issues of the publication. See the "Idea" above. Cut and mount the photos as described in the student project option.

Part II

Using the students' "_____ Photo Search" activity sheets, create and distribute a one-page handout for students that has on it all the information about the five countries/regions researched. For an example see the activity sheet in this section entitled "Photo Search Challenge." If the teacher preparation option is chosen in Part I, this is the activity sheet to be copied and distributed to students.

Hang up the photos around the classroom.

Using the information on the "Photo Search Challenge," students match the photos with the correct country/region by placing the number of the photo in the matching box. The teacher may begin the lesson by reading one description aloud while students follow along, then sending the students to search for the photos that match only that country/region. Reconvene the class after a time limit and have the group who researched that country/region reveal the correct answers. If the teacher prepared the photos, he or she reveals the answers. Allow students to defend other choices they made. If the defense is reasonable, accept the answer. Some photos could have characteristics that would indicate another appropriate choice in the matching. The photo search is on when students fully understand the activity. Allow students enough time to study the photos and descriptions and to discuss and debate with friends over correct matches.

Wrap up with an answer session that includes a discussion of human-environment interaction. Ask the class what kinds of stereotypes are created with this kind of lesson, pointing out, for instance, that not all people in the MidEast wear white robes. End with a discussion of how the physical features and climate in your area affect the way students and their families live.

Other ideas: Students do photo essays of human-environment interaction in their area.

Distribute one *National Geographic* magazine to each student. The student finds a photo that shows an example of human-environment interaction and shares it with the class. For students to fully explain their photos, they may need to do a little research to understand the topography and climate of an area.

Name _____

_____ **Photo Search**

Group names: _____

_____

Directions: Research the country or region named above to complete the information below.

CLIMATE:

_____

_____

_____

_____

PHYSICAL FEATURES:

_____

_____

_____

FLORA AND FAUNA:

_____

_____

_____

_____

OTHER ENVIRONMENTAL INFORMATION:

Name _____

Photo Search Challenge

Directions: Below are environmental descriptions of five countries or regions in the world. Hanging in the classroom are numbered photos from each of these five places. Match the photos to the places by putting the photo number in the box that corresponds with the country or region where you think the photo was taken.

THAILAND

CLIMATE: tropical
Three seasons: spring - hot and dry, 98°
                  summer - hot and wet, 98°
                  winter - mild, 62°
In the mountains it is cooler in the winter, 32°, but still 90° in the summer. Monsoons occur in the summer; heavy rains cause flooding.

PHYSICAL FEATURES: mountains, valleys, rivers
The rivers are used extensively for transportation and irrigation of fields. The rivers form a series of canal systems in many towns.

FLORA AND FAUNA: tropical fruits, flowers, trees
The country is famous for its exotic hardwoods, spices, and animals.

SWITZERLAND

CLIMATE: mild; affected by altitude:
valleys, plateaus - winter, 29°, snow
                  summer, 65°–70°
mountains - winter, 15°–20°, snow
           summer, 50°–60°

PHYSICAL FEATURES: the Alps, a high mountain range
The Alps are covered with snow in the winter; melting in the spring adds to many rivers, lakes, and streams. Plateaus and valleys are well irrigated and have grassy fields in the spring and summer.

FLORA AND FAUNA: over 3,000 varieties of flowering plants and many hundreds of kinds of trees

MIDDLE EAST REGION

CLIMATE: hot and dry
The Arabian Gulf is one of the hottest places on earth with an average temperature of 100.4°. The mountains, because of altitude, in some parts of the Middle East will get cold in the winter.

PHYSICAL FEATURES: desert, rivers (many of which dry up in the summer)
In some places you can get water only by digging.

FLORA AND FAUNA: oases, palm varieties
There are some large fertile oases on which towns are built.

KENYA

There are three distinct regions in Kenya: plains, fertile highlands, tropical coast.

CLIMATE: Plains: dry, 60°–80°
          Fertile highlands: mild, rain, 67°
          Tropical coast: tropical, 80°

PHYSICAL FEATURES: Plains: extensive flatlands, some hills, cover 3/4 of the country
Fertile highlands: hills, mountains
Tropical coast: beaches, coastline

FLORA AND FAUNA: Plains: short bushes, trees, scrub grass, variety of animals
Fertile highlands: grass, trees, bamboo, variety of agricultural products—coffee, corn, sugarcane, tea, cattle

ICELAND

CLIMATE: summer - cool, 54°
          winter - mild, 31°
          autumn - rainy, windy

PHYSICAL FEATURES: coastline, mountains, glaciers cover 12 percent of Iceland, rivers—which may be fed by melting glaciers, earthquakes, geysers, volcanoes, hot springs

FLORA AND FAUNA: Grassy plains—good for grazing sheep. Iceland used to be covered with trees but they were mostly destroyed for housing and firewood in early settlement years. The people are replanting in an effort to protect Iceland from erosion. The country also contains over 150 species of fish and over 250 species of birds.

Capital E for Endangered

Objective: Students will identify the main threats that endanger wildlife species while becoming familiar with 10 specific species and the problems surrounding their survival.

Preparation: There are 10 "Species I.D." cards that match with 10 "Why Am I Endangered?" cards. The answers are provided on the bottom of the description cards for the teacher. Make note of which ones match and fold the name under or cut it off at the dotted line before copying the cards for students. Cut apart, mount on construction paper, and laminate each card for lasting use. Copy two "Capital E for Endangered" student sheets for each student.

Procedure: Shuffle the cards and randomly distribute to students, ensuring that each card's match has been distributed. Have students complete as much of the "Capital E..." sheet as they can using the information on the card. Students then mingle, looking for the person who has the match for his or her card by sharing the two descriptions and comparing information on the student sheet. Once a match is established, those students should sit down to share all additional information with one another so they can complete the "Capital E..." sheet. If a student is sitting, it indicates that he/she has matched up, narrowing the options for those still searching. As the sheets are completed by the pairs, students may uncover inconsistencies in the match and realize they need to stand and mingle again. Some of the species are similar in some ways.

When all the matches are identified and "Capital E..." sheets completed, students read aloud concerning their endangered species. After each pair shares, the teacher should ask the class to identify the main reason for the endangered status, making a list on the board. When the list is complete, go back and ask students which species are endangered because of human interaction with the environment. Point out that although all are endangered because of man, most may also be saved from extinction by human intervention.

When discussing the populations of the animals it is helpful to give students some comparisons for size. Although 10,000 of some species may sound like a lot, compare it to a human population of over five billion.

Many state universities have approximately 10,000 students. What if those 10,000 were the only people left on earth? Some are too old to bear children; some cannot conceive; some are ill; every year a percentage dies. It takes almost a year for just one baby to be born. Add to that equation the notion of decreasing habitat or a relentless predator and students can begin to see how fragile a population of even 10,000 can be. If students are ready for the complex concept of a healthy gene pool, bring this into the discussion. Lead into the question "How do we protect species not only from extinction but from being endangered in the first place?"

Other Ideas: Have pairs prepare posters displaying their species including a picture of the animal, a fact sheet, and a strategy for protection.

Students could develop an advertising campaign for the preservation of their species. Encourage the use of a variety of media including the newspaper, magazines, radio, television, and public demonstration. If the projects are exceptional, consider asking a local cable station to run the ads.

Have students write to local, state, or national organizations for information on endangered species.

Show movies about endangered species, available for rent at libraries and video stores. The more students can identify with the creatures who are threatened, the more they will want to do to protect them today and in the future. They must be provided with visual images of these animals in their habitats.

Follow up: Ask students to prepare more cards by doing a research project on an endangered species. They may use the "Capital E..." sheet as a research guide. Do the activity again with the student-generated cards.

Vicuña

This wild relative of the domesticated llama is the size of a deer with a long neck, a light brown coat of soft wool, and a bib of white on its lower throat. It lives like a goat in herds, up in the high altitudes of the Andes. At one time, this animal populated the mountainous regions of South America in the millions. With hair seven times as fine as human hair, though, it was overhunted very quickly once it was discovered. The early Spanish settlers liked its meat as well as its fur, so by 1825 there were already pleas to protect it from extinction.

Spectacled Bear

The only species of bear found in South America, the spectacled bear inhabits the slopes of the Andes mountains. White markings around its eyes give it a raccoon appearance, as if it is wearing glasses. It climbs trees and eats vegetation, fruit, and buds. Occasionally, if times are tough or if provoked, it will kill and eat another animal.

Why Am I Endangered?

Between being a tasty morsel for early settlers and providing a sumptuously soft, fur rug, each of these animals was well worth the hunt to those in need or those with greed. The early 1800s found this animal already threatened with extinction. Numerous attempts were made to pass effective laws protecting this species, but still in 1957 over 400,000 of these animals were destroyed. In 1965, only 10,000 survived in the world. Efforts to raise this animal in captivity are still experimental. If herds are raised domestically, the wool can be sheared every two years without killing the animals. This will drastically reduce the need for poaching to obtain a fleece.

Why Am I Endangered?

Another species threatened by encroaching agriculture, this animal can only hope that advancing farms do not climb too high up forested mountains. Considered a menace by farmers raising livestock, these animals are shot on sight without thought of their impending doom. The distinct fur markings also make them great targets for hunters.

Vicuña

Spectacled Bear

Chinchilla

The bushy-tailed chinchilla has the honor of having thick, 1" long, pearly blue-gray fur, flecked with black. It looks much like a cross between a field mouse and a gray squirrel. Living in the mountains of Bolivia, Peru, Chile, and Argentina, these animals congregate in large, burrowing groups. There used to be three wild species, but the "royal" chinchilla is now believed extinct in the wild.

Volcano Rabbit

This creature looks like a huge mouse with big ears. It lives only at altitudes of 9,000 to 12,000 feet and is known to exist only on Popocatepetl and Ixtacihuatl, two dormant volcanoes south of Mexico City. The zacaton grass that grows in the rich volcanic soil is its favorite food. These animals live in colonies and burrow tunnels similar to those of common rodents.

Why Am I Endangered?

In the city of Coquimbo, Chile, 217,000 pelts from this animal passed through customs back in 1905. In 1909, less than 28,000 managed to find their way to the border. Hunted almost to extinction for $40 each, this animal is prized for the making of fur coats. In the early 1900s a coat made of this animal sold for $100,000. Today skins range from $15-$45 each because most are raised in captivity and are plentiful. In the wild however, the species numbers are highly diminished.

Why Am I Endangered?

There were only about 1,000 of these creatures left in the early 1970s. Even though much of the area where they live is within national park boundaries, there are private companies who own some of the slopes they inhabit. These slopes have especially fertile ground and are being developed for farming. Hunters, until quite recently, would use these small animals as target practice.

Chinchilla

Volcano Rabbit

Quetzal

This is one of the world's most spectacular birds! Mostly green, with a gold shimmer to its feathers, the quetzal also has a bright, ruby red breast. The Aztecs and Mayas considered the quetzal sacred and never killed it. They did, however, capture the male of the species and pluck the long tail feathers, four-foot plumes, to use in headdresses for priests and rulers. The birds were then released to grow another set of plumes. Quetzals live in the cloud forests of Central America. Making their homes in the holes of trees, they can raise two to four offspring per year.

Why Am I Endangered?

This bird was hunted to rarity by the early Spanish settlers. The feathers were used for the fancy bonnets of rich women in Europe. After Guatemala made this species its national bird, emblazoning it on coins and stamps, the species was able to recover a bit with protection laws designed to save it. More threatening than the early hunters, now the farming industry destroys the forests and trees the animal calls home. To save this magnificent bird and still continue with economic growth, artificial nesting boxes are supplied and more national parks have been established.

West Indian Parrots and Macaws

These brightly colored birds live in Latin America, including the West Indies, Central America, and the Amazon region of South America. They are native to tropical rainforest areas. Christopher Columbus' son wrote about "red parrots as big as chickens" on the island of Guadeloupe in 1496. Now that island has no parrots at all.

The macaw is bigger and more colorful than its relative. While the parrot will cost $100 to $1500 in pet shops, macaws' prices range in the thousands. This is because they are becoming more difficult to find and many must be smuggled into the United States at a high cost to those dealing in illegal trade.

Why Am I Endangered?

These animals inhabit rainforests. They are now less common and even non-existent on many islands in the West Indies where they were once plentiful. Hunting and habitat destruction were the first causes of their declining population but now a new threat has been added to that list. People want them as pets and are willing to pay high prices for them in pet shops. As many as 57,000 were smuggled into the United States in 1976. Of those, 9,000 died on or before arrival. For every one that is sold in a pet shop, 4,000 have died on the way. Although they are intriguing and funny, people are encouraged not to purchase these animals anymore unless a thorough background check can positively confirm the origin of the animal.

Quetzal

West Indian Parrots and Macaws

Giant Galapagos Tortoise

Once abundant on the Galapagos Islands in at least 15 different varieties, the giant tortoise now comes in only 11 varieties. The total population of the tortoises on the islands is between 6,000 and 10,000. The tortoise eats the sparse vegetation that grows in the volcanic soils. Once hatched, the young are vulnerable to attacks by cats, rats, and other scavengers. Many do not survive. If they do, they grow to weigh up to 500 pounds and live for a century or more.

Why Am I Endangered?

These animals probably might have been spared had their limited habitat not become a human settlement. When man arrived, he brought goats and pigs which ate much of the vegetation on which this animal depends. They ate so much of the food, in fact, that man soon realized that this place was not suitable for colonization. Homesteads were deserted leaving much of the livestock behind. The habitat of this species cannot support large meat-eaters, and soon, without any natural enemies, the goats and pigs overpopulated. Once scientists realized the impact of the goats and pigs, they were removed in hopes of helping wild animals recover their once thriving existence. One race of the species, the Isla Pinta, was considered extinct until 1971 when "Lonesome George" was found. Still living, he may well be the last of his kind as no others have been documented. The other races are doing better with continued support.

Giant Galapagos Tortoise

Golden Lion Tamarin

A member of the monkey family, the golden lion tamarin is a fun-loving red-squirrel-sized marmoset that lives in trees eating fruit, berries, insects, and small lizards. There are three varieties of this tamarin—the golden lion, the golden headed, and the golden rumped. The long yellowish-orange hair covers the golden variety completely, whereas the other two are black with gold only appearing as their names suggest. There are approximately 200 of each variety left in the wild, a total of 600 in all.

Why Am I Endangered?

This animal is adamantly sought as a pet because of a cute face, small size, and a good nature. Zoos clamor for one to display, but there are not many to be found. Captive breeding is becoming more successful, however, and international attention to this animal's highly endangered status may help save it. The limited habitat in the coastal Brazilian rainforest is threatened by human development, especially since this part of the forest is so much more accessible than the inner reaches of Brazil. The wild variety of this species is a hairline from being considered a hopeless case for survival. Scientists hope to help repopulate the wild colonies by releasing captive animals if experimental breeding continues to be a success.

Golden Lion Tamarin

Giant Otter

The giant otter, measuring from five to six feet in length, is the largest of all otters in the world. It lives in slow-moving rivers where it can eat fish and shellfish, swim, and play all day long. The giant otter has a chocolate-brown fur and lighter-colored throat. It is a very gregarious animal, living in social groups where play is more fun and sharing is common. Currently the highest population of this animal is in Surinam, where protection goes back to 1954.

Jaguar

The largest of the wild cats in the Western Hemisphere, the jaguar can reach lengths of eight feet and weights of 250 pounds. This cat is the ruler of the jungle, known to kill livestock and even people who wander into its territory. Decorated with a beautiful yellow or light brown coat with black spots, the jaguar is well camouflaged in the thick forests that are its home. It roams from Mexico to Argentina but is most densely populated in the Amazon area.

Why Am I Endangered?

One of the five most endangered species on earth, this mammal's pelt brings up to $50.00. Never having an abundant population to begin with, the furs from this animal killed in Peru in 1946 numbered around 2,000. In 1960, by contrast, only 200 pelts were reported in the trade market. In 1973, Peru put a ban on hunting the creature, as had neighboring countries already. But smuggling of these pelts is still occurring. The La Plata variety of this species is also extremely close to extinction. These two water mammals, the tiger, and two varieties of leopard are the five animals with the dubious distinction of a total and indefinite ban on their fur trade. Their species could easily be gone forever in the next decade without absolute cooperation from humankind and mother nature alike.

Why Am I Endangered?

This animal is killed on sight by many of the people who come in contact with it. The species is feared because of its power and stealth and pursued because of the value of its luxurious coat. People in the United States bought 23,000 pelts from this creature in 1968 and 1969 but only 7,000 in 1976. The government of Brazil is giving the species some protection from hunting but not doing enough to protect its habitat. In fact, poacher danger to this animal is now surpassed by the increasing habitat destruction from which this animal suffers. This species will fight for survival as long as the rainforests continue to be destroyed. It needs a large hunting area to support its needs and will not reproduce if it feels that the space of its surroundings are unsuitable for raising young.

Giant Otter

Jaguar

Name _____

Capital *E* for Endangered

Directions: You have been given one card of a two-card match. Using the information on your card only, to begin with, fill in as much of the information below as possible. Proceed by finding the other student who has your match. Together, complete any remaining blanks on this sheet. Some of the information asked for below may not apply to your species; fill in the blanks that are appropriate for the species you were assigned.

Endangered Species Fact Sheet

Identification of the Species (Name): _____

Physical Description and Characteristics of Behavior: _____

_____

_____

_____

_____

Food Source: _____

Description and/or Location of Habitat: _____

_____

_____

_____

_____

Reason for Endangered Status of the Species: _____

_____

_____

Most Current Population Estimate: _____

_____

Pack Your Bags

Objective: The student will apply knowledge about the environment to the human experience.

Preparation: Make five copies of each information sheet found with this lesson. Fold accordion-style on the dotted lines to imitate a brochure style handout. Add some color to the drawings if time allows.

Copy enough "Pack Your Bags" student sheets for each student to have one.

Obtain encyclopedia volumes that include Colorado, Barbados, Thailand, and New England (or at least one of the states mentioned in the brochure).

Procedure: After introducing the theme of Human-Environment Interaction, set the stage for a pretend travel club meeting. Tell students they are members of the club, attending the meeting to plan for their next vacation. Randomly distribute one brochure and one "Pack Your Bags" sheet to each student.

Inform students that their brochures describe the trips they will be taking. Give them five minutes to brainstorm a list of things that they will need to take on their trips. They should write these on the "Pack Your Bags" sheet.

Form groups that have similar brochures, for example, a "Trek to New England" group would meet in one corner of the room and a "Trek to the Jungle" group would meet in another corner. Give each group a clean copy of "Pack Your Bags" and the appropriate encyclopedia.

In each group have students select the following:

1 recorder–to write down items to pack on the "Pack Your Bags" sheet
1 researcher–to look up climate and other information in the encyclopedia.
3 readers–to split the task of reading the brochure and the packing list aloud to the class.

Groups compile one master list of what to pack for their trips by sharing ideas they generated previously. So that everyone has a chance to contribute, the group could go around their own circle taking turns giving ideas. Set a time limit for finalizing the list; start with 10 minutes and extend it if needed. If one group finishes before another, encourage that group to find some climate and topographical information to share from the encyclopedia.

When everyone is done with the packing list, it is time to share as a whole class. As the readers share their brochures and packing lists, the teacher challenges items students think they need, asking how the environmental conditions affected their decisions. The goal of the lesson is for students to understand that the environment and humans must interact successfully to survive together in a healthy way.

As a starting point, some items that students should have on their lists or consider when packing are listed below.

New England—Cool nights, warm days, light load for mountain trekking, bug repellent, sleeping bag, extra bike gear for a flat tire or a breakdown on rough mountain trails, and hiking boots.

Rockies—Cold nights, warm days, light loads, winter camping gear and wear, instant heat packs for cold hands and feet, chapped-lip ointment, sunscreen, and sunglasses.

Barbados—Warm nights, hot days, sporting equipment, swimsuits, beach shoes, hat with a brim, sunscreen, and sunglasses.

Jungle—Hot nights and days, rain gear, a few pairs of shoes, bug repellent, camera, first-aid kit, and long sleeves and pants so branches will not scratch.

Did any of students on the jungle, ski, or mountain biking treks think of bringing a container in which to transport their garbage out of the wilderness?

Pack Your Bags

Directions: Read the travel brochure describing the imaginary trip you are about to take. Based on the information you have from the brochure, plan a packing list of what you will carry in your luggage or your backpack. Write down the things you will bring in the luggage outlines below.

Trek to New England
FALL FOLIAGE FUN

This one-week trip takes you through three New England states—Maine, New Hampshire, and Vermont. You will feast your eyes on the spectacular splash of color offered by the autumn leaves while hiking in the Green Mountains, taking a train ride in the White Mountains, and mountain biking in the Appalachians. Come ready to breathe the cool, fresh air that fills New England as the leaves turn.

Accommodations:

Saturday - Monday: Camping on the Trail

Tuesday and Wednesday: Mount Washington Resort Hotel

Thursday - Saturday: Chimney Pond Cabin at Mt. Katahdin

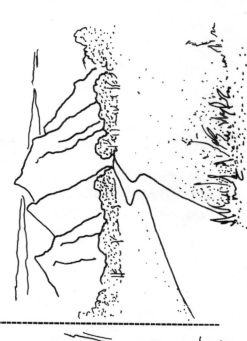

Date of Trip:

October 12 through October 19

Provided:

* food and drink

Bring:

* camping equipment
* mountain bike (rentals are available)
* appropriate clothing and other items

Trek to the Rockies
A WINTER WONDERLAND OF SURVIVAL

During one week of incredible back country skiing, you will experience the wonder of the Rocky Mountains in winter. The pristine wilderness will become your play yard as you make your way from Loveland Pass, Colorado, to Grand Junction, Colorado. Your trip will take you right through an animal migration route sure to provide a wildlife watcher with the thrill of a lifetime.

Accommodations:

Saturday: Keystone Cabins at 12,000 ft.

Sunday - Wednesday: Camping

Thursday: Up Creek Lodge, a full-service facility

Friday: Vacation Inn at Grand Junction, Colorado

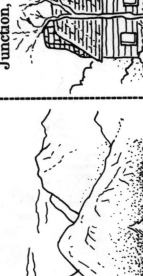

Date of Trip:

April 14 through April 21

Provided:

* food and drink

Bring:

* camping equipment
* skiing equipment
* appropriate clothing and other items

Note: You will be carrying your own equipment on the journey; plan accordingly.

Trek to Barbados
ISLAND ADVENTURE

Date of Trip:

July 3 through July 10

Provided:

* food and drink
* windsurfers and surfboards

Bring:

* camping equipment
* sporting equipment (excluding those items mentioned above)
* appropriate clothing and other items

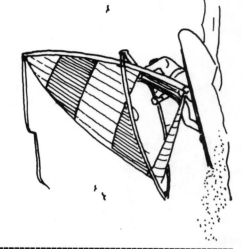

Spend a whole week soaking up the rays of this friendly island while participating in a water sport adventure. On the Atlantic coast you will have a chance to windsurf and catch some waves on a surfboard, if you dare! The Caribbean shore offers a gentle breeze for more sailing, coral reefs for snorkeling, and sunken pirate ships for scuba diving enthusiasts. Local Barbadians will gladly take you parasailing, waterskiing, and jet skiing, too!

Accommodations:

Saturday - Monday: East Point Lighthouse Campground with your host Alvin the lighthouse curator

Tuesday - Friday: Crystal Beach - an all-inclusive resort

Trek to the Jungle
A MALAYSIAN MYSTERY TOUR

Find yourself surrounded by the mystery that is the jungle in this one-week excursion for the daring soul who loves the unknown. Join a group of local trackers as they lead you searching for the elusive tiger, the Asian elephant, and the giant python—who is sure to grab your attention! Since tracking is most successful in mud, the rainy season is the optimal time for this journey into the jungle.

Accommodations:

Saturday - Thursday: Platform Camping in the Jungle, locations to be announced

Friday: Bangkok Gardens Resort

Date of Trip:

June 17 through June 24

Provided:

* platforms for camping
* food and drink
* elephant porters for equipment
* animal-attack protection equipment

Bring:

* camping equipment
* appropriate clothing and other items

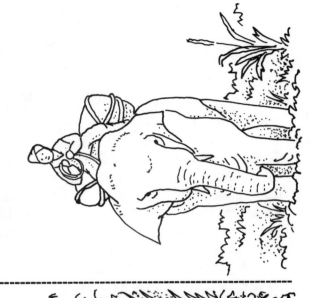

CHAPTER FOUR

REGIONS

To understand other places around the world, one needs a frame of reference, a way to compare and contrast. Each of us, because we have a *place* that we live, has at least one point of view from which to see other places. A person who has traveled has an even broader perspective. Educators commonly approach the study of geography by dividing the world into its political boundaries, facilitating learning about countries. This method can be effective only to a point, because many unifying bonds which places share are not within these political borders. The world can be defined in terms of **regions** as well, physical and cultural characteristics which make places alike and different.

Tokyo, Japan, and Detroit, Michigan, are alike. They are both automobile manufacturing regions. Tokyo, Japan, and Detroit, Michigan, are different. Tokyo is a highly Shinto region; Detroit is a highly Christian region. Both of these examples are defining a region with human characteristics.

Physical features can also be a manageable way to compare places. The Himalayas of Asia and the Andes of South America, the two highest mountain ranges in the world, have something in common. But even though they are both mountainous regions, the Andes are much closer to the ocean and experience a milder climate than the inland Himalayas. The Andes are in a fairly productive agricultural region; the Himalayas are not.

Regions can change over time due to changes in climate, economic conditions, accessibility of trade routes, and many other factors. Geographers study how regions change to predict the needs of the people and the effects on the environment. The theme of regions is important in terms of our learning to manage the differences and similarities which allow our world to function as a unit.

The Big Book

Objective: Students will apply knowledge and research of regions to compare local and global communities.

Preparation: Obtain a few copies of the picture book *People* by Peter Spier. Public and school libraries carry this book, as do many bookstores. This activity lends itself nicely to multi-age work. If you want to do this project with a lower grade teacher, for example first grade, as a multi-age activity, arrange meeting times for the students in both classes.

Gather the following materials: large sheets of white drawing paper, coloring utensils, scissors, glue, construction paper, and craft odds and ends such as feathers, straw, felt, sequins, toothpicks, and yarn.

Procedure: Introduce the theme of regions using your own ideas and/or the ideas from this chapter's introduction. Regions give us a way to compare and contrast places. Read the book *People* by Peter Spier to the class and show the pictures.

The task of students will be to design a big book much like Spier's creation, with a twist. There will be 10 sections to the book and each will have two pages—a local page and a global page. If you are working with a lower grade on a multi-age project, the younger students will design the local pages and the older students, the global pages. If you are keeping this as a classroom project, pairs will contribute to both pages.

Pair the students and have them choose one of these 10 sections:

> clothing, recreation, homes, holidays, foods, religions, pets, land forms, languages, races

The pair must design one page that shows the common or majority local interpretation of the section. They must also create a page that shows some global interpretations of the section. For example, if the section is on pets, the local pets might be dogs, cats, birds, and fish. The global section might have snakes, elephants, monkeys, and llamas. Each page is the size of a poster sheet of white construction paper and should be 3-D wherever possible. For instance, the pet shapes could be cut out of felt with movable eyes glued on; birds could have colored feathers attached.

On the global pages it is necessary to write the area of the world from which the idea came under the picture created. For some, regions may be defined instead of countries. For example, there may be a group of representations on desert-region homes, including a tent and an adobe home. Then there may a group of representations on cold-region homes, including a Swiss chalet and an igloo.

Pairs can make up a sentence to go with each page, such as those found in the *People* book.

Some pairs may choose to put a map on their global page to highlight regions of focus. Some may use well-known, stereotypical ideas and others may delve into subtleties of culture. Encourage students to do some research on regions of the world, look at *National Geographics* for ideas, and use the *People* book as a resource.

The goal of the activity is for students to learn something new about regions of the world and apply the knowledge in a creative way. When the pages are done each pair shares their part of the book. There will be much new information for the class in this activity. Global awareness is developed. It is interesting to see students discover how much cultural diversity the United States really has and how easily we may stereotype other places. The teacher can lead a discussion on these two topics when the project is complete. You do not think all Arctic people live in igloos, do you? And certainly, not all Africans eat chocolate-covered ants, right?

Other ideas: Display your "big book" in the school library as a wall exhibit. Or bind it and share it with elementary students.

People everywhere need a home.

Homes are different everywhere.

Multiple Identities

Areas of the world are commonly identified by political boundaries, but there are many other ways to characterize places. This lesson concentrates on regional characteristics that give places multiple identities. Combining all these identities would give students a more complete picture of a place.

Objective: Students will be able to recognize areas of the world in terms of their regional features.

Preparation: Make up 3" x 5" cards, each one containing a regional characteristic. Use human and physical features, such as religion, government, language, climate, and land forms. Also, on each card draw a simple key symbol. Here are some examples:

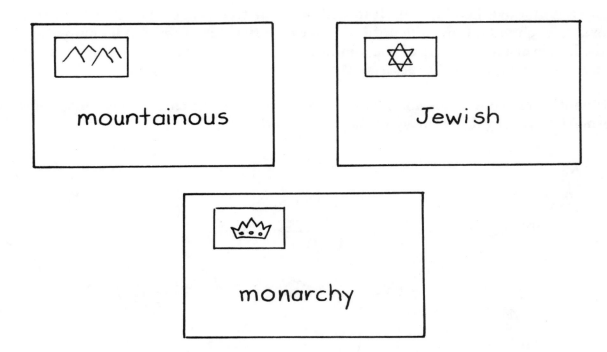

Copy overhead transparencies of the world outline map found at the back of this book. Make one transparency for each category used on the cards. The teacher should have one blank map overhead for religions, one for governments, and one for land forms.

Copy enough world outline maps onto paper so that each student has one.

Procedure: Each student selects one card at random. Having students pair up is an option to consider. Using encyclopedias or other research materials, a student looks up his/her feature and finds out where it is prominent in the world. He/she should select one or two places where the feature occurs. On his/her outline map, the student draws the symbol for the feature where appropriate. This should take only a short time. If the teacher wishes, students might also jot down some information that describes the characteristic on the card selected.

Gather the class back together. Project a blank map overhead onto the wall or screen and select one category to begin the activity, for example, religion. Have the people who researched religious characteristics come up to the overhead one at a time and draw the symbols of each religion in the locations they identified. With religions, for instance, the overhead would have symbols for Islam, Judaism, Christianity, Buddhism, and other religions. This one overhead would generate discussion since three of these are prominent in the MidEast. It becomes clear why this region is in turmoil.

Put up another overhead and fill it in with symbols from one of the other categories, for example, climate. Continue until all the categories have been drawn onto overheads. Lay overheads on top of one another to graphically demonstrate how one place can have many regional characteristics.

If students took some notes about the characteristics on the cards, they could share the information as they draw the symbols on the overheads.

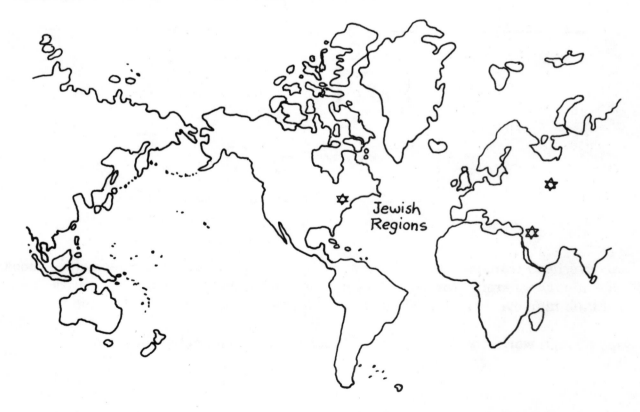

Regional Reasoning

Objective: The student will use deductive reasoning skills to determine regional identities.

Preparation: There are three regional narratives included in this lesson and a list of 10 possible places where these narratives might take place. The lesson asks students to read a narrative, identify regional aspects of the place described, and determine which of the 10 places is the setting of the story. The teacher might choose to have all three narratives randomly distributed to students or to work on one narrative at a time as a class. Choose one of these options and make the appropriate number of copies of the narrative(s).

Copy one "Regional Reasoning" student sheet for each student. Plan to conduct this lesson with the use of encyclopedias, the *World Almanac,* and other resource books that include information on the 10 countries listed on the "Regional Reasoning" sheet. Another option is to implement this lesson in the library where these resources are available.

Procedure: (See choices in "Preparation" section above. This procedure details the second option, working together as a whole class.)

Distribute one narrative and a "Regional Reasoning" sheet to each student. Ask students to read the story. Using the student sheet, have them identify regional features mentioned in the story. Review the findings so that all students have a complete information page from which to work.

Maria Gonzales   Martin Bodin   Abdul Gupta

Direct students to the list of 10 countries found on the "Regional Reasoning" sheet. The task is to determine in which country the story takes place. Looking at a physical map of the world, help the class to narrow down the options. land forms are the most obvious regional feature to determine.

Once the choices are limited to three or four places, have students use the other information on the sheet to deduce the answer. They achieve this by looking at the "Facts in Brief" boxes that encyclopedias provide under each country's listing or by looking in the *World Almanac,* a wonderful resource for this lesson. Some students will have cultural literacy of their own to apply in the reasoning process. Once students have figured out the country in question, ask them to keep it to themselves in order that others can continue the search on their own. Those who finish more quickly can try another one of the narratives.

Narrative #1 is set in Brazil, #2 in Sweden, and #3 in Nepal.

Follow up: Assign one of the remaining seven countries to each student. He/She can write a story, modeled after those provided, about someone in that country. Suggest that he/she complete a "Regional Reasoning" sheet about the country first and then include some of that information in the narrative he/she will write. More than one student will be working on the same country. It may be an opportunity for pairs to create a piece together.

When the stories are completed, exchange them among the class members. Let the students use "Regional Reasoning" to figure out which country is the setting for each story. Share them aloud and post them on a bulletin board that has a map on it. Run yarn from each story to its country of origin.

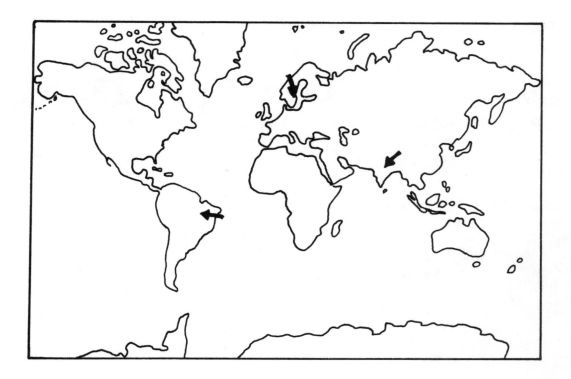

Regional Reasoning–Narrative #1

Maria Gonzales, age 11, awakes at dawn to the sound of her mother making *cafezinho,* a sweet, hot coffee, to be served in tiny cups before the family leaves for the sugar cane fields. They must get to work early before the tropical heat makes midday work too uncomfortable. Maria does not go to school because the government cannot provide a teacher for public education in her area. Her father attended school in a big city as a child; he can read and write and tries to teach Maria in the evenings.

Maria's family is very close. All of her relatives live in the same neighborhood as she and her parents. They all work in the fields or stay home with their young children. Further away, in the wealthy part of town, Maria has seen children going to school, not only to learn subjects but to learn the dances and songs for *Carnival.* This is an important holiday with a parade that celebrates the music, art, and culture of her country. She cannot go to learn the dances formally but she practices with her friends anyway.

On Sundays she always attends a Catholic church down the street. Then she usually plays soccer with cousins and friends. The field where they play was once a cane field and before that it was rainforest. She likes the social time at these games. She has met a boy who one day she hopes to marry. Although many girls in urban areas wait until they are in their twenties to marry, it is common for rural girls to take a husband as early as ages 12-15. This boy has talked about owning his own farm. The government gives away land to those who will move out into the rainforest, helping to build the road as they move. Maria would miss her family but is excited by the adventurous opportunity.

Martin Bodin is planning a vacation from his usual work in a steel factory. He and his wife, who also works, will take their children and go to the coast for two weeks. They have saved quite a bit of money despite the high taxes they must pay in their country. One reason they have been able to put money away for vacation is that child care for working mothers is free. With two incomes, they can afford to get away for two of the four weeks they have off from work. Friends of theirs, who live in an apartment next door, are going with them.

They plan to relax on the white, sandy beach for much of the time, letting the sun bleach their already blond hair. The resort island offers much in the way of sightseeing, also. They will visit the Viking museums, the walled city of olden-day knights and horses, and the gardens that cover the grounds of public parks. It is warmer in the southern part of the country than it is where Martin and his family live. They enjoy mild summers from May to September, but snow flies even in June sometimes. It will be nice to get away and the smorgasbords will be the finishing touch on what promises to be a wonderful vacation.

Martin's oldest son has a holiday from school. He has finished his second year of compulsory education and will attend for eight more years, until he is 16. Then he may choose to go to the university, which is free to national citizens, or enroll in the armed services. Some, but not many, young people begin work at 16 and do not choose either of these options. Frederic thinks he would like to be an American exchange student for one year to practice his English. It is required that all children learn English from the time they are seven until they finish school.

Frederic is looking forward to vacation also. He is bringing his bicycle and soccer ball. Keeping physically fit is important to him. The people of his country take pride in their health. Since the health care system is free to everyone it is logical to have frequent checkups. Any health problems are often discovered before they become serious. People do not like their high taxes but they are well cared for and well educated. People in Frederic's country have the highest standard of living on the continent. From the rolling fields they grow much of their own food. From the rivers they generate most of their own hydroelectric power. From the Lutheran church they gain much unity as a people. The Bodins are happy here.

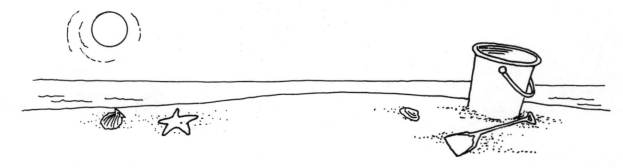

Abdul Gupta is a bit nervous today. He is getting married. His parents, in the Hindu tradition, have arranged for him to wed a girl from another village. They are in the same *caste*, of course, meaning that they were born into the same social class. It is very uncommon for Hindu people to marry outside of their caste. Abdul's life is already planned for him. He will be a farmer, like his father, working in the sugar cane fields. He will build his own house of brick, stone, and mud. Although he has heard of others in his caste leaving for jobs in the city, he is not educated enough to pursue this option. Like 70 percent of all people in his country, he did not go any further than sixth grade.

Abdul's mother is busy preparing for the celebration. Family gatherings are very festive and entertaining. She lays out the clothes she will wear, a brightly colored blouse and long skirt. Her husband's best knee length robe and black pants are ready, too. The wedding will take place in an ancient temple, artfully decorated and full of the reverent nature of the Hindu people. The party will be here at the modest house overlooking a mountain valley. Behind them the jungle looms and the mountains rise high into the clouds. It appears to be another hot summer day in the hills.

Mrs. Gupta will need to go to town to pick up some supplies. She can find almost all she needs in the bustling village marketplace. Many times she cannot understand the vendors; there are so many languages and dialects spoken in her country that it would be impossible to know them all. At least 12 languages and 36 dialects are common. One of the things Abdul wanted at his party was a seafood appetizer. This his mother cannot find at the market today. It must not have come with the trading shipments this time. She will make Sherpa tea with butter and salt, rice cakes, and cornbread, but no seafood appetizers. She is disappointed; hopefully, Abdul and his wife will find some in the city when they travel on their holiday. As she makes her way home she thinks of her son, wishing him good luck and many children in his marriage. This is a special day.

Regional Reasoning

Directions: Read the story provided and look for clues that will help you to fill in the information asked for below. Look at the list of 10 countries at the bottom of this page. Using an atlas and other resources, determine which country is the setting of your story.

Physical Features/ Land Forms _____

Climate _____

Major Religion _____

Industry _____

Education _____

Government _____

Cultural Aspects (Traditions, Interests, Dress, Food) _____

_____

_____

Use a deductive reasoning process and the regional characteristics discovered above to determine which of these countries is the setting of your story:

Nepal   Brazil
Canada   United States of America
Peru   Japan
India   Cuba
Sweden   Kenya

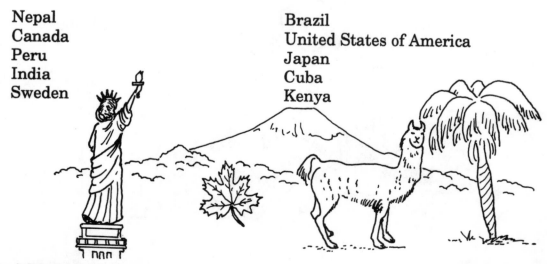

Foreign Funology

Objective: Students will identify different regions of the world according to the languages spoken.

Preparation: Make an overhead transparency of the world outline map found at the back of this book. The teacher may choose to do 10 tracings of this map onto poster-sized paper ahead of time or let students do the tracing.

Obtain as many foreign language dictionaries as possible from libraries and personal collections. Ask parents to lend copies they may have at home.

Provide coloring utensils.

Procedure: Pair students and give each pair a poster-sized world outline map. Give each pair a common word or phrase, such as those listed here:

Happy Birthday, Hello, Goodbye, Thank You, I Love You, Mother, Father, One-Two-Three, Happy New Year, Nice to Meet You

The pair must find out how to write this word or phrase in at least five different languages. Select the number of languages according to how many dictionaries you can obtain.

The students write the foreign word or phrase on the poster map where that language is commonly spoken. If there is more than one place that the language is common, they put it all places. For example, Portuguese is spoken in Portugal and Brazil. Encourage students to research the languages of different regions to be able to locate the words in as many regions as possible. Europe will get very crowded but that will make the point that Europe is a multi-lingual region.

Students share their posters, trying to pronounce their words correctly to the class. The class may want to repeat the words, also.

Ideas:
- color code each language
- use glitter glue to write
- display in foreign language classrooms

CHAPTER FIVE

MOVEMENT

The earth is populated by 5.5 billion people. Most of us depend on other people from many different places to provide us with products and information. There is an intricate system of movement for things to get from one place to another, things such as food, clothing, and resources. Not only tangible things move in this system though. Thoughts, ideas, and information travel all around the world and affect the lives of people everyday. A look at technology is a large part of the study of **movement**.

When considering the theme of movement as a way to study geography, one should ask these five *W* questions: Who, what, where, when, and why do things, people, and information move? Also, how do they move? There are patterns of movement which make our lives in the United States predictable and orderly. Sometimes these patterns are interrupted and people feel a ripple effect from the system breakdown. Many countries, however, do not have a pattern of movement to depend on and this can worsen things such as famine or wartime relief efforts. To some, it is a welcome change to find a place that is not easily accessible to the flood of information and imports that drive the economic world.

Movement is very important to the study of geography because it can contribute to the development of the human characteristics of a place, such as cultural traits, governmental practices, and tolerance of diversity. Physical geography is a strong determinant of patterns of movement, dictating how easily roads can be constructed and shipping lanes supported. Sharing of products and ideas links the people of the world. Students should be able to determine how movement connects them to the many regions and resources close to them and miles and miles away.

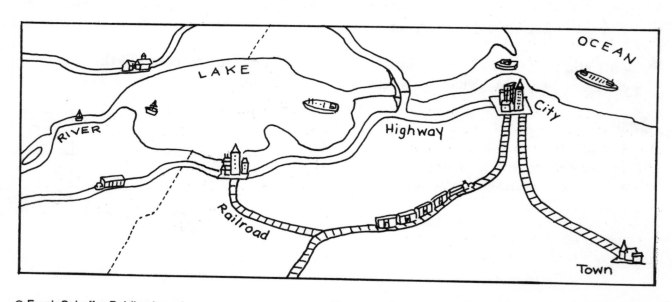

Look at the Label

Items in the classroom can easily represent a microcosm of the world economy. You will be surprised how many countries are represented on the "Made in..." labels of products in your classroom. This lesson makes students aware of the global economy needed to furnish and outfit their classroom and themselves. It challenges them to find "Made in..." labels from as many countries as possible.

Objective: Students will become aware of the interconnectedness of the world through trade.

Preparation: Hang up five large pieces of chart paper around the room. Label each with one of the following: clothing, equipment, books/paper products, small supplies, other.

Copy for each student a "Look at the Label" sheet for data collection at home. Have chart paper ready to label and hang.

Procedure:

Part I

Call students' attention to the chart paper hanging around the room. Tell them that you want them to survey the classroom for these different items, looking at the "Made in..." labels. Assign students to groups or let them choose groups. The teacher needs to decide how the survey will be done. He/She may assign a certain kind of item to a group of students or a certain section of the classroom to a group. When students find a "Made in..." label on an item they should record the name of the item and the country in which it is made on a piece of paper. When the group has surveyed all the items they were assigned, each student in the group should take a turn writing an item and country of origin on the appropriate chart paper in marker.

Students should look at their clothing tags, bookbags, notebooks, pencils, rulers, and other items.

When the data collection is complete, gather students to process the information. This can be done in a few ways:

1. Groups are asked to organize data from each chart by country. For example, one group is assigned Japan and counts all items made in Japan, using all the charts.

2. Groups are asked to organize data on just one chart. For example, one group works with the clothing chart, listing all countries mentioned and how many products are from each of those countries.

3. The class works as a whole, categorizing data in one of the two ways described above.

The teacher can ask students to make graphs of the data. Here are some examples.

- Make a bar graph showing the different kinds of items made in Mexico.

- Make a bar graph showing all the different countries from which the small school supplies in the classroom came.

- Make a pie graph of the percentages of books printed in the various countries named.

The teacher may choose to process information using generalizations rather than specific data. "There are more supplies made in the United States than in Japan, but more equipment made in Japan than in the United States."

If the classroom has a world map, put dots or tacks on it to indicate all the countries represented in the survey of classroom products. Discuss how the theme of movement is demonstrated in this lesson. What would the classroom be like if international trade did not exist or was restricted? What effect does a trade restriction have on a country? Why do countries impose trade restrictions?

Part II

Challenge students to find product labels from as many countries as possible by looking at home. Distribute a "Look at the Label" sheet to each student for homework. For other kinds of items, brainstorm with students possible products that they can look for at home to check the labels. These might include kitchen gadgets, tools, furniture, and toys.

The next day, gather the information for the challenge and place a sticker or push pin on each country represented in the home data. Sharing the data from home can be a lesson in cooperation. Ask students questions and see if they can come up with the answers without teacher suggestions. Once they have an idea as to how they will interpret the data, the teacher may facilitate their efforts.

Possible questions:
How can the class get a good idea of the distribution of all the products surveyed? (Do they want to put up chart paper again?)
Do most of the families in your classroom have a foreign automobile? What products are being made primarily in the United States of America?
What generalization can be made about watches?
How many people in this class would have a television if it did not come from Japan?

Here are some brand names and their countries of origin to assist in identifying items that do not have a "Made in . . ." label accessible.

Televisions	**U.S.A.**: RCA, Zenith **Japan:** Quasar, Sanyo, Sony **Netherlands:** Magnavox
Stereos	**U.S.A.**: Radio Shack/Realistic, RCA **Japan:** Hitachi, Panasonic, Sanyo, Sony, Technica, Toshiba
Cameras	**U.S.A.:** Canon, Kodak, Polaroid **Japan:** Konica, Minolta, Nikon, Olympus, Pentax
Watches	**U.S.A.:** Elgin, Texas Instruments, Timex **Japan:** Seiko
Cars	**U.S.A.:** American Motors, Buick, Cadillac, Chevrolet, Chrysler, Dodge, Ford, Lincoln, Mercury, Oldsmobile, Plymouth, Pontiac **Japan:** Nissan, Honda, Suburu, Toyota **France:** Peugeot **Germany:** Audi, BMW, Mercedes,Volkswagen **Great Britain:** Jaguar, MG, Rolls Royce **Italy:** Fiat **Sweden:** Saab, Volvo
Bicycles	**U.S.A** Schwinn **Japan:** Mishiki, Univega **France:** Peugeot, Motobecane **Great Britain:** Raleigh

Look at the Label

Directions: If you have these items in your home, look at the labels on them and see where they are made. Write down the brand names, also. There is space for two of some items in case you and your family have more than one! If you have more than two, write the others down on the back of this sheet.

Brand name   **Made in . . .**

Television

Camera

Watch

Automobile

Refrigerator

_____

Look all around your house at as many labels as possible. If you find an item made in a country not yet identified in class, write it down.

Kind of item   **Brand name**   **Made in . . .**

Use the other side if needed!

Keep in Touch

Information travels quickly nowadays with the technology and networking available to average people, not only those in high-ranking positions or of great wealth. Besides word of mouth, the mail used to be the only way that information traveled long distances. Due to geographic obstacles, like a mountain range or an ocean, some information took a long time to reach its destination. Growth of our nation was dependent on the mail and still is in many ways, especially economically. How information and ideas move in and out of a place is an important way to describe what a place is like. This lesson introduces, through skits, the history of the United States Postal Service as a way of considering how information moves.

Objective: Students will use the history of the mail as an example of how information moves, increasing their understanding of the theme of movement as it relates to information and cultural development.

Preparation: Each skit has parts to be spoken. Make enough copies of each skit so that each person in the skit can have his/her own copy of the script. Provide props as necessary.

Procedure: Divide students into groups of appropriate sizes for each skit. Give each group enough scripts so that each member has one. Students select actors for each part and practice their skit. Each group performs its skit for the class in a succession that follows the time line of the history of the mail.

After the skits are performed, write this prompt on the board:

It is the year 2025; the mail moves much more quickly. Letters can be sent and received in one day. How is this accomplished?

Students work with their groups to create a new skit based on the future of the postal service. Have students perform their skits for the class.

Lead a discussion on what it would mean to the average person to have the mail move more quickly. Incorporate thoughts on how it would affect student research, corporate billing practices, personal mail, and the mail-order business.

The Postal Boy of Babylon

Person 1: I am entrusted to carry this clay tablet to the king of Babylon. It was finished today, June 23, 2000 B.C., and must be delivered by the end of July.

Person 2: But that is miles from here, over the mountains and the desert. How will you do it?

Person 1: I am fleet of foot and have much courage. I am strong and can manage the 100 pounds of this tablet. It is for the king! I will drag it and be there in just a few weeks.

Person 2: Good luck, Postal Boy of Babylon. If you do not make it, I will know you are dead, for nothing stops the mail!

****

Postal Pony Boys of Persia

King's Servant: Postal Boy, take this bronze tablet, written today, September 21, 600 B.C., to the royal residence.

Postal Boy: I will need a swift horse at each post, my master.

King's Servant: It is arranged. The horses will be waiting.

Postal Boy: I am off with the tablet. Nothing will delay the mail. *(Person 2 rides a horse across the room, stopping at a post where Person 3 is standing.)*

Horse Boy: *(Saddling a horse)* Postal Boy, here is your fresh horse. You are making good time on your journey.

Postal Boy: *(Dismount first horse and climb onto second)* Thank you, Horse Boy. This is a fine horse. I hope the next two posts have as fine a horse for my journey.

Horse Boy: *(Waving as Person 2 leaves on horseback)* They will, Postal Boy, it is a royal route, after all. And nothing stops the mail!

****

The Courier and the King

King Louis XI of France: Courier, come here!

Courier: Yes, Your Highness, King Louis XI.

King: I need a message delivered to my high court officials in Paris. It must arrive before the new year of 1452 begins. It is Christmas Day, is it not?

Courier: Yes, Your Highness, I am your servant. I will have a swift royal horse at each post and will arrive in Paris within the week.

King: Rest when you arrive, Courier. This must be delivered without delay. Sleep only when you are so tired that you will fall off your horse without sleep. I am counting on you and severe punishment, even death, may be the consequence if you tarry.

Courier: *(Gallops away)* Yes, Your Highness, I am able to travel seven miles an hour in the summer, but only five in the winter. I will make it five and a half miles per hour today if it kills me.

Common Person: *(Hail the courier to stop.)* Stop, Courier. I need you to deliver this message to my sister in Paris.

Courier: You fool, I cannot stop for such a commoner. The mail service is much too expensive for you. Only the highest ranking in society can afford it. You do not have enough money to make me delay my route.

Common Person: You just wait, Courier. In 100 years everyone will be able to afford the mail. I can see into the future.

Courier: If you want your letter delivered 100 years from now, I'll be glad to see it is if I'm still alive...Ha ha ha.... *(The courier rides off, laughing.)* After all, nothing will stop the mail.

****

Richard Fairbanks and the Penny Delivery

Judge in General Court of Massachusetts: *(Sitting behind a judge's bench in a courtroom.)* On this day in 1639 I decree that all mail coming from abroad be delivered to Richard Fairbanks of Boston. He has a system for delivering the mail and it will no longer be held by the town office until someone picks it up.

Richard Fairbanks: *(In the courtroom)* I am proud to provide this service and I can make a living, too. Thank you, Your Honor. *(Leaves the courtroom and goes home)*

Delivery Person: Here is a sack of letters from the ship that just docked from England, sir. *(Hands over a heavy bag of mail, then leaves)*

Richard: Thank you. *(Richard looks through the sack and then sorts the letters.)* I will sort all those going south toward New York in one pile, another pile for those going north toward Maine.

Delivery Person: *(Returns to Richard's house)* I am here to pick up the mail to be delivered. It has been two days; is it sorted?

Richard: Yes, here you are. This is for the southern route. Don't forget to get one penny for each letter delivered. And remember, nothing will stop the mail.

****

Skit 5 of 10 **The United States Postal Service Is Born** Three Parts

British Officer: Mr. Benjamin Franklin, I have a message for you from the British Crown offices.

Mr. Franklin: What is it, sir?

Officer: You have been working for the postal service here in the British colonies of the New World since 1737; that is 37 years, Mr. Franklin.

Mr. Franklin: Yes sir, that's true.

Officer: You have now become sympathetic to the wishes of the colonists to be free from British rule. You are allowing mail that talks of rebellion to pass through the postal service. We cannot let this continue. You are fired.

Mr. Franklin: I will accept this release with pride. I believe in freedom and it won't be long before the colonies are free, you will see. *(Turns back to the audience and walks away.)*

(American official enters and stands at a podium. Franklin reenters and faces the official.)

American Official: I, the head of the Continental Congress, on this twenty-sixth day of July, 1775, appoint you, Mr. Benjamin Franklin, as head of the American Postal Service. We must operate as if we were a free country, for soon we will be, no doubt!

Mr. Franklin: Thank you, sir. I will make the American postal service dependable and swift. Nothing will stop the mail.

****

Skit 6 of 10 **Train Tracks and Postal Sacks** Two Parts

Engineer: Here comes the postal carrier. Start the train; we are off on our route. From Maryland to Ohio, from New York to Georgia, we deliver the mail.

Postal Carrier: I see you have a train load of passengers today.

Engineer: Yes, we are doing a great business now that the postal service uses our trains for delivery. We make enough money by delivering mail to lay new tracks all the time.

Postal Carrier: That's great; it keeps me busy, too! Say, do you think there will be railway service all the way out West soon?

Engineer: Who knows. Not many people living out there yet.

Postal Carrier: Well, the news of gold in the hills will surely attract many to head out that way. They will need to send word of their success back East to the families they leave behind.

Engineer: How true. It takes a long time to lay tracks, though. Wonder what they'll do until the railroad reaches the Pacific? *(Thinks for a few seconds.)* Well, I have to get this train moving. Nothing can stop the mail, you know.

****

From Sea to Shining Sea

Postal Worker: You're a gold miner, aren't you?

Gold Miner: Yup and I've struck it rich! I'm sending a letter home to say that I'm coming back a wealthy man. *(Waves a letter in his hand.)* It's about time; been here for five years, since 1852.

Postal Worker: It will take a while to get there, ya know. It has to be hand carried to the Columbia River boat, go down the river to the Pacific mouth. It will be loaded on a ship bound for Panama where it will be given to a hand carrier again. He will bring it across Panama to the steamer that will carry it back to South Carolina through the Atlantic. When it gets there the railroad will take it as near to your hometown as possible. A hand carrier will deliver it to your post office where your wife can pick it up. *(Shows the route on a classroom map if possible.)*

Gold Miner: Sounds like quite a journey. I might be home before my letter at that rate.

Postal Worker: No, Sir. That route is still quicker than a journey across the Rockies and the prairies. I do hear, however, that stagecoaches are delivering mail from St. Louis to San Francisco starting next year.

Gold Miner: You boys are always thinking of something. Seems like nothing can stop the mail.

****

Alaskan Mail Delivery

Postal Dogsled Driver: This mail is going from Kotzebue to Barrow. *(Show the route on a classroom map if possible.)*

Postal Worker: Are you sure you can make it? These bundles weigh 700 pounds!

Dogsled Driver: It will be difficult to get it there before the holidays this year, 1892. It is 650 miles of cold and wind, but nothing stops the mail. *(Mushes the dogs and drives away.)*

(New scene on other side of the classroom)

Postal Worker: Charles, it is so exciting that you can do what you love and get paid for it. So few have this job right now, but if it works out, think of the jobs it will create.

Charles A. Lindbergh: I can't believe I will be flying mail to people in such a short time. Think of how quickly people will get their mail now.

Postal Worker: I have a friend in the Alaskan postal service who will be very happy to learn to fly the mail from Kotzebue to Barrow instead of taking a dogsled team.

Lindbergh: It is only an experiment, remember. But I think that by 1918, air delivery of the mail will be a scheduled service.

Postal Worker: We really mean business when we say:

Together: Nothing stops the mail.

****

Skit 9 of 10   **The Pony Express**   Four Parts

Senator William M. Gwin of California: Listen director, your freighting company–Russell, Majors, and Waddell–stands to make a lot of money if you implement my idea for faster mail service. The people who will use it want to get word home as soon as possible that they have discovered gold. They want their families on stagecoaches right away, so they can start enjoying the wealth of their claim together. It's 1860; by 1861, you will be rich from such a simple mail service.

Director of Russell, Majors, and Waddell Freighting Co.: Senator Gwin, how do you expect mail to get from Sacramento, California, to St. Joseph, Missouri, in 10 days when a stagecoach can only travel that distance in three weeks?

Senator Gwin: My idea is to shorten the route by 160 miles, going off the California Trail in places. Stagecoaches have to follow the trail due to rough terrain, but I figure that a man on horseback could easily traverse some of the mountain passes of the Rockies and the Sierra Nevadas. If the men could ride at a steady gallop for 15 miles, then switch horses and ride another 15 miles, I think they could cover over 200 miles a day. The route is 1,900 miles long so 10 days should do it for one route.

Director: We'll try it. Let's advertise in the newspaper for Pony Express riders. We can hire 100 and see how it works. We will charge $5.00 for each half-ounce of mail. The riders will carry 20 pounds on each ride. You are right, Gwin, we will be rich and the mail will reach between East and West in record time. We will be rich and famous.

(New scene on other side of the classroom)

Mother: Do you think this Pony Express thing is a good idea, son? It sounds dangerous and difficult.

Pony Express Rider: I'm young, in shape, a good rider, and a sharp shooter. I'll ride like the wind; I'll take on those Indians and wild animals. I'll ride day and night, through sandstorms or blizzards. It's an adventure and I'm being well paid, $100 a month.

Mother: I'm so proud of you, son. Now, take your Bible, your knife, your horn, your rifle, and your pair of Colt revolvers that were issued to you by the company and deliver the mail.

Pony Express Rider: *(Jumps on horse)* I'm off on the Pony Express.

(Back to other scene)

Director: Senator your idea is working. The men can go 250 miles per day, the whole journey in eight or nine days. Of course, we did have to lighten the load to keep up that pace.

Senator: What do you mean? There are still 20 pounds of mail delivered on each trip; I weighed it myself the other day.

Director: Of course, Senator. The men carry only one revolver now. We lose only a few a month to the Indians and other hazards. It's working quite well, but it will be short-lived, I'm afraid. The telegraph should be wired from Missouri to California by November 1861. Oh well, we all knew that nothing could stop the mail.

****

Skit 10 of 10   **Modern-Day Mail Service**   Two Parts

Postal Worker: How would you like that sent, first- or second-class?

Customer: Will first-class get it there by tomorrow?

Postal Worker: No, not to California from Missouri. First-class would take three or four days probably.

Customer: How about two-day service? How much does that cost?

Postal Worker: That is $2.90. That means it gets priority but two days is not guaranteed, just attempted.

Customer: And overnight?

Postal Worker: Ten dollars for overnight service. It will be on a jet and delivered to the receiver's door tomorrow.

Customer: Overnight service, please. Here's a 10-dollar bill.

Postal Worker: I wonder if same-day service is next. How could we possibly guarantee that?

Customer: I'm sure the postal service will find a way. Nothing stops the mail.

****

Shipments for Sherlock

This activity addresses the theme of movement with a problem-solving approach done in cooperative groups. At first glance it may seem difficult to implement but in taking the time to read a scenario and walk through the procedure ahead of time, the activity becomes very systematic. It is an effective lesson worth the time to read, understand, and try with students.

Objective: Students will use problem-solving skills and cooperative efforts to demonstrate an understanding of the theme of movement.

Preparation: Plan groups of four purposefully to include a heterogeneous mix of students. Assign each student one of the four roles described below based on his/her strengths. It may be helpful to make a poster-sized chart of the descriptions for each role.

Copy the "Shipments for Sherlock Scenarios" pages and cut along the dotted lines, separating the "scenario" section from the "vehicle" section. Copy enough world maps for each student. Provide each group with coloring utensils, scissors, glue, and student atlases.

It may be helpful to read through each scenario and map out a possible route. Making a poster of the rules may be useful for the class as well.

Roles

reader–reads the "Shipments for Sherlock Scenario" and the rules to his/her group whenever necessary

locater–uses the atlas to find cities and marks them on the outline map

ruler–measures distances and determines scale miles; draws route and records distances

driver–cuts, colors, and glues vehicles on the route

Procedure: Assign students to their respective groups of four and tell them the title of the role they will fulfill for this activity. Give each group one scenario, one strip of vehicles, and the other materials described above.

Read these directions to the class:

"You are groups of Sherlock Holmes detective assistants. Each group has been given a problem to solve. Each person in the group has a specific role to perform, but all of you will discuss the problem and its possible solutions. When you are finished, you will present your solution to the class. Listen carefully to how you are to perform your task. Please wait until I have completed giving directions before beginning your work.

One of you is the **reader**; he/she will read the scenario aloud to the group to start the activity and will reread the problem or parts of it as needed. Each scenario asks you to determine a route of travel from one city to another, while transporting a certain product. You are determining a trade route and what kind of transportation vehicles are needed to follow that route successfully.

Once the **reader** has shared the problem, the **locater** has the job of finding the involved cities in the student atlas. He/she will then find the approximate locations of those cities on the world outline map given to the group. The **locater** will put a star and label where each city is located. Others in the group may help the **locater**.

The group will then look at the physical world map in the student atlas and find a realistic route to get from one city to the other. There are also some rules you must follow in solving the problem. They are described in the scenario.

To determine the route and follow the rules, one of you, the **ruler**, will measure distances using the scale found in the atlas on the world map page. (The teacher may need to meet with the **rulers** ahead of time to brush them up on interpreting scale distances. Assigning this role to a student who is adept at this skill is helpful.) The distances will help you determine which vehicle to use to transport the goods. The **ruler** draws the path the route follows onto the world outline map and makes a note of distances.

The **driver** colors the vehicles and cuts them out. He/she glues the appropriate vehicles on the different sections of the route. (This role is appropriate for a lower-level learner.) This completes the problem-solving part of the activity. When groups are done with this we will share our routes. You may begin."

The teacher should float around to the different groups to facilitate the problem solving, give ideas, and reinforce the sharing of the work by staying in the roles assigned.

When the groups are finished they should have a route with distances recorded drawn on their outline map. Vehicles of transport should be glued on in appropriate locations. The groups then share their scenario and solution. Divide the sharing as follows:

reader–reads scenario to class

locater–shows all cities involved and traces route for class to see

ruler–describes distances between each stopping point

driver–introduces the vehicle used at each interval of travel

Anyone in the group can interject with explanations of why they chose a certain route, obstacles avoided, and other problems that were overcome. The teacher should ask students to explain their decisions.

Shipments for Sherlock–Scenario #1

Lima, Peru, is a leading exporter of sardines. The president of Kenya is holding a benefit fund raiser with a guest speaker who loves sardines. The president has ordered sardines as the appetizer for this event, which will be held in Nairobi. With other orders
from Recife, Brazil; Lagos, Nigeria; and Addis Ababa, Ethiopia, the exporter figures he
can make the deliveries all in the same trip. You have been hired by the sardine company to plan the trade route. There are certain rules for you to follow in reaching the
destination:

*You must use all four forms of transportation, even if it means going out of your way
to accomplish this feat.

*You must use the vehicles as follows:

Freighter–used for all ocean or sea travel, distance unlimited
Barge–used for all river travel, must not go a distance of less than 200 miles or more
            than 1000 miles
Train–used for all overland travel of 1,500 miles or more
Truck–used for all overland travel of 1,499 miles or less

*You must stop in all the cities named in the scenario, beginning at Lima and ending
at Nairobi.

*You must choose what you believe to be the shortest route.

- -

Shipments for Sherlock–Scenario #2

The teen-agers of New Delhi, India, are very keen on Levi jeans. They are demanding that stores stock the item. The best deals on the item come from the original plant in San Francisco, California. Stores in New Delhi have placed an order and are waiting for the merchandise to arrive. Levi Strauss & Co. has other stops to make on this delivery route which include Boston, Massachusetts; Rome, Italy; and Mogadishu, Somalia. You have been hired to plan the trade route for Levi Strauss & Co. There are certain rules for you to follow in reaching the destination:

*You must use all four forms of transportation, even if it means going out of your way to accomplish this feat.

*You must use the vehicles as follows:

Freighter–used for all ocean or sea travel, distance unlimited
Barge–used for all river travel, must not go a distance of less than 200 miles or more than 1000 miles
Train–used for all overland travel of 1,500 miles or more
Truck–used for all overland travel of 1,499 miles or less

*You must stop in all the cities named in the scenario, beginning at San Francisco and ending at New Delhi.

*You must choose what you believe to be the shortest route.

- -

Shipments for Sherlock—Scenario #3

A specialty shop in Brisbane, Australia, carries famous Swiss chocolate from the city of Geneva. The owners have just opened another store in Melbourne, Australia, and need stock for both stores as soon as possible. The Swiss company, Edelweiss Chocolates, is delivering to stores in Beijing, China, and Singapore, also. The branch in Brisbane wants Edelweiss distributors to stop in Brisbane first so they can unload some of the chocolate and send the rest to Melbourne. Edelweiss has hired you to plan the trade route. There are certain rules for you to follow in reaching the destination:

*You must use all four forms of transportation, even if it means going out of your way to accomplish this feat.

*You must use the vehicles as follows:

Freighter—used for all ocean or sea travel, distance unlimited
Barge—used for all river travel, must not go a distance of less than 200 miles or more than 1000 miles
Train—used for all overland travel of 1,500 miles or more
Truck—used for all overland travel of 1,499 miles or less

*You must stop in all the cities named in the scenario, beginning at Geneva and ending at Melbourne.

*You must choose what you believe to be the shortest route.

- -

Shipments for Sherlock—Scenario #4

A Japanese automobile distributor in Dallas, Texas, is running short of the Suburu Legacy four-wheel drive station wagon. The compact yet versatile car has become popular for use as a family vehicle on a ranch.

The distributor needs to receive a shipment immediately from Suburu's plant in Tokyo, Japan. Suburu has many distributors to supply and needs to stop in Anchorage, Alaska; Winnipeg, Manitoba; and St. Paul, Minnesota. You have been hired by Suburu to plan the trade route. There are certain rules for you to follow in reaching the destination:

*You must use all four forms of transportation, even if it means going out of your way to accomplish this feat.

*You must use the vehicles as follows:

Freighter—used for all ocean or sea travel, distance unlimited
Barge—used for all river travel, must not go a distance of less than 200 miles or more than 1000 miles
Train—used for all overland travel of 1,500 miles or more
Truck—used for all overland travel of 1,499 miles or less

*You must stop in all the cities named in the scenario, beginning at Tokyo and ending at Dallas.

*You must choose what you believe to be the shortest route.

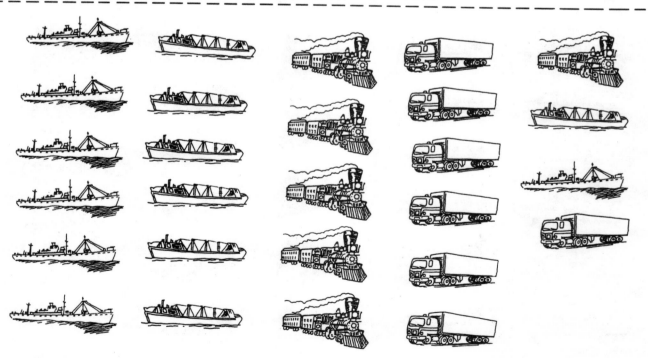

Shipments for Sherlock–Scenario #5

Honolulu, Hawaii, is hosting one of the stops on the international tour of "The World's Most Famous Gems." The exquisite sapphire exhibit comes from Colombo, Sri Lanka's national museum. The exhibit must travel with the world gem tour to Johannesburg, South Africa; Brasilia, Brazil; and Caracas, Venezuela, before arriving in Honolulu. You have been hired by the International Museum Commission to plan the touring route for this exhibit. There are certain rules for you to follow in reaching the destination:

*You must use all four forms of transportation, even if it means going out of your way to accomplish this feat.

*You must use the vehicles as follows:

Freighter–used for all ocean or sea travel, distance unlimited
Barge–used for all river travel, must not go a distance of less than 200 miles or more than 1000 miles
Train–used for all overland travel of 1,500 miles or more
Truck–used for all overland travel of 1,499 miles or less

*You must stop in all the cities named in the scenario, beginning at Colombo and ending at Honolulu.

*You must choose what you believe to be the shortest route.

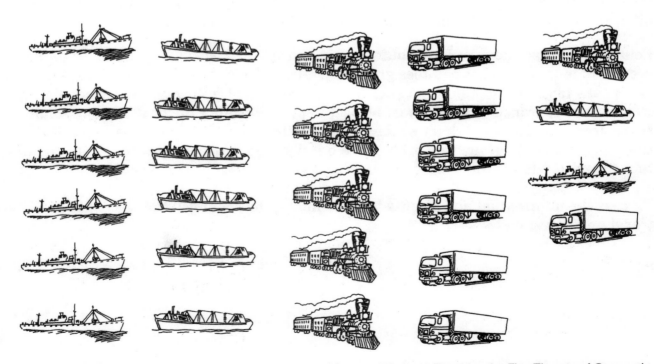

Move It

People and products must move to keep our world connected. Things change more rapidly now than ever before because transportation and communication are so immediate. The world economy depends on transportation. A place that does not have people and products moving in and out is not able to keep up with developments. How well things move in and out will be important in terms of defining a place.

Objective: Students will demonstrate an understanding of the history of transportation and create new ideas for the future of transportation.

Preparation: Part I requires no preparation. For Part II, copy the "Move It" student sheets so that each student will work on one of the seven. There will be more than one student, for example, working on air travel. The teacher may decide to have seven groups, each working on a different mode, instead of assigning individuals to the various modes.

Write the list of "Ways to Deliver the Message" on the board or copy it onto an overhead. Provide coloring utensils, construction paper, scissors, and glue.

Procedure:

Part I

Begin by discussing movement as a theme in geography. See the introduction of this chapter for some thoughts on this. Have students generate a list on the board of any possible modes of transportation they may have heard about or experienced. The teacher may want to do a survey of how many students in the class have used these different modes. Students can develop a bar graph using this data.

Point out different geographical routes and scenarios on a world map. Some examples are: "You must transport potatoes grown in Ireland to southern Italy" or "You have two weeks to go on vacation from your home in Maine to California." Ask students which mode of transportation would be best in accomplishing the goal. Eliminate air travel from the choices. Ask for explanations for their choices. Give some "what ifs" that may change their answer, such as, "What if a road was not cut through this mountain range?" "What if there were no motorized vehicles yet?"

Process the information and discuss how technology has changed the possibilities for travel and movement.

Part II
Randomly distribute the seven different "Move It" student sheets, one to each student. Provide the list "Ways to Deliver the Message" on the board or on an overhead projector. Students must tell the class about their mode of transportation in a creative way. Give students time to read the information and select a delivery method. Have them follow the directions on the instruction sheet.

Each student delivers his/her message on the history of one mode of transportation by reading aloud the piece created. Ask the class to reiterate the important points, evaluating how well the student incorporated the historical information.

After all have shared, distribute scissors, construction paper, and glue. Students cut and mount their messages on construction paper with drawings of their vehicles. They may cut and paste the drawing provided if they choose. Hang the drawings in the classroom as a display on the theme of movement.

Follow up: Have students design and share new modes of transportation in the form of models or drawings. Add them to the display.

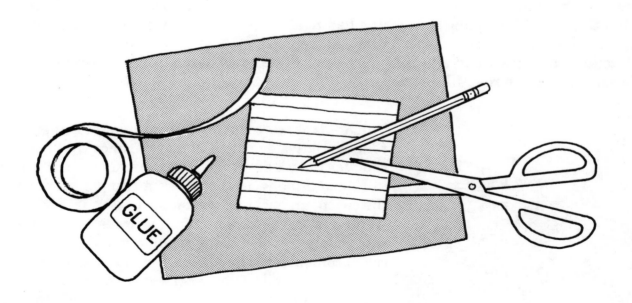

Move It by Foot or by Beast

When people in primitive times wanted to travel or move things it meant walking. They dragged heavy loads behind them or carried many small loads until all the goods were moved. Later, animals carried people and bundles on their backs. Sleds were the next step, allowing animals to pull the heavy loads instead of teams of men. Oxen, camels, dogs, donkeys, reindeer, and elephants were used in their respective parts of the world. Many are still in use today as beasts of burden. The horse was one of the last to be trained. It was not until the A.D. 900s that the horse collar was invented, making the horse useful in pulling heavy loads. Also in that century, horseshoes were created, saving the tender hooves of the creatures as they performed tasks that are unknown to the wild variety of horse.

Move It by Wagon and Coach

The Sumerians in western Asia were probably the first to use the wheel. However, it took hundreds of years to be seen as valuable because there were no roads on which to travel. The wheel was not useful on uneven or unpredictable surfaces. But, as early as 100 B.C., the Chou dynasty in China had roads. They were so busy that traffic rules were instated, including a speed limit. All vehicles with wheels were wagons pulled by humans or animals and all roads were basically narrow paths trodden many times to wear them into a road-like surface.

The Romans were the finest road builders, needing reliable routes on which to move armies that hoped to conquer the world. Some Roman roads are still in use in England today. In the 1400s, a Hungarian invented the coach, an enclosed wagon for passengers who wanted to travel. Two hundred years later, Europe was widely traveled along regular routes by stagecoach companies. They had set points, called stages, for pick up and drop off. At the stages, people and animals would rest and eat. In 1756, the American stagecoach went from Philadelphia to New York. Homesteaders moving their families West invented the covered wagon around this same time.

Move It by Ship

The surface of the water is much smoother than that of land; there are no trees, no mountains, and no sandy or muddy areas. Centuries before the wheel was invented or animals were domesticated, boats were traveling on the Nile. Sheep and goat skins tied over logs made a water-worthy raft. Hollowed-out logs propelled with long poles that pushed off the bottom were the first canoes. Later the paddle and oar were created and after that the sail. Large ships called galleys were used by the Phoenicians as trading vessels from the Mediterranean Sea to the British Isles. These ships carried more than goods; the people aboard spread great amounts of knowledge and custom as they traveled. They also spread diseases previously found only in remote parts of the world.

Ships were used by the Romans to invade foreign lands. The sailing ships went faster with the triangle sail invented in A.D. 500. In 1200 the compass was put into use, making it possible to go away from the sight of land and not get lost at sea. Explorers were more daring with this development and colonization of distant lands became more realistic. Trade flourished and faster boats were needed. The clipper ship with its many sails was invented by Americans around 1840 to trade with Europe.

Move It by Water–Steamboat and Diesel Engine

In 1787, American John Fitch invented the steam engine and introduced it on a steamboat. People teased him about it, not realizing the potential of such a creation. The Civil War put a hold on inventions but soon after it ended, iron ships replaced the wooden whaling and clipper ships. For a while the steamboat was popular, especially for river travel. Then, propellers and the turbine engine replaced the paddle wheel and the sail.

In the 1900s the diesel engine came into use. The ocean liners that began operation in 1870 using steam, now used diesel fuel. Passengers could travel across the ocean on vacations.

The large ships carried cargo and people, performing two services in one trip. It seemed like the perfect business that would never end. How else would people get across the ocean, after all? Of course, when the airplane was perfected, ocean liners as a mode of transportation were rendered obsolete. The cruise ship business, as a vacation in itself and not a way to get somewhere, is coming into its prime just now in the late 1900s. Boats are mainly used for pleasure and shipping, not for travel.

Move It by Railroad

The first railroads did not have engine-powered trains on them; they had horse-drawn carts on wooden rails that hauled coal and iron ore out of mines. The first steam engine to run on tracks was invented by Richard Trevithick in England in 1804. It was not a dependable rig, breaking down frequently and using enormous amounts of fuel to produce steam enough to power it. But it was still less expensive to fix and run than it was to feed a horse or replace it due to injury or overwork. Only 21 years later the engine had been improved enough to run passenger service on the Stockton to Darlington line in England. Five years later in 1830, the first United States rail service opened, running from Maryland to Ohio. This development put the stagecoach virtually out of business. Roads were neglected from non-use until the automobile came into the picture.

Today, trains are diesel or electric for the most part. Their use in freight hauling is widely accepted as most efficient. In Europe, passenger service is still a popular mode of travel. The United States is coming back to trains as a more economical, environmentally friendly form of transportation. Maglev trains are the newest variety of trains, designed for passenger service. They are a magnetic levitation vehicle that actually does not touch the track. No friction means high speeds are possible, giving these trains the ability to travel up to 200 miles in one hour. Besides being fast, they do not create much pollution at all.

Move It by Automobile

Henry Ford is credited with the first practical automobile, but the attempts of others paved the road to his success. In the late 1700s there was a steam-powered car that did not catch on. In the late 1800s, a German put a gas-burning engine in an automobile but no one paid attention. In the early 1900s, an electric car was invented, but the battery needed charging every few miles. Charles Duryea made the first gas-engined car in the United States but it was flimsy, made using bicycle tires. Only wealthy people could afford to run it and keep it repaired. It was not the car as much as the assembly line that made Henry Ford a success.

In 1908, Ford invented the Model T, assembled on line and available in 1913. People could buy it at an affordable price and since they were all alike, parts were easily obtained when they broke down. Almost 15,000,000 Model Ts were sold before 1927. This availability truly changed the way Americans lived. People could work in one town and live in another. They could travel for pleasure, not just out of necessity. Tons of jobs were created in manufacturing, road building, fuel processing, and many related retail businesses. The automobile continues to be the most important vehicle of movement in existence.

Air travel began in France with the hot air balloon in 1793. By 1900, there had been countless attempts by backyard inventors to fly with the use of a steam or gas-powered engine. Flying machines were fashioned after birds and insects, but they were not successful until December 17, 1903, when the Wright brothers took the first engine-powered flight at Kitty Hawk, North Carolina. By 1936, the Douglas DC-3 was in operation, carrying 21 passengers on the first commercial flight in history. It could travel 170 miles per hour. The average plane in 1958 went 300 miles per hour. Also, in 1958, the jet was introduced at 500 miles per hour. The helicopter appeared in 1947 and with these two inventions, transportation and warfare changed forever. Fortresses with walls higher than a mountain could not keep an airplane out. Ocean liners with 20-day passage across the Atlantic could not compete with the airline's one-day service. Flight capability changed the world, opening trade talks between countries, making it possible to ship perishable foods, and allowing mail to reach people in a timely manner.

The 1976 Concorde jet, flying from Paris to New York in just a few hours, was the first look at "fantasy travel." Being able to go across an ocean to a foreign country for lunch and be back home for dinner was no longer impossible. The pollution, fuel consumption, and noise created by the Concorde leaves much to be desired, though. The newest look at air travel is the TAV–Trans-Atmospheric Vehicle–a hypersonic aircraft that flies 10,000 miles per hour at 100,000 feet. It might be in commercial use by the year 2000, meaning one could fly from New York to Tokyo, half way around the world, in less than two hours! It is the future "Orient Express" fueled by hydrogen and oxygen, emitting water vapor, not fumes.

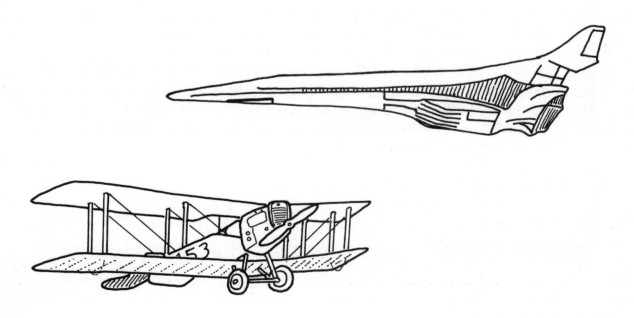

The following paragraphs present an overview of transportation information for use in presenting this section to students.

At first people traveled only on land, by foot. River travel was soon discovered as a quicker route and primitive boats were developed. Domestication of animals as beasts of burden was the next successful step in moving people and things. As people began to settle further and further apart, and sailing ships were built, seaports became popular. The first major cities were built around seaports so that trade and colonization could occur. With the quest for land, moving inland became necessary, bringing about the need for covered wagons and stagecoaches. The railroad was built soon after, making passenger service and freight hauling a relatively quick and efficient mode of transportation. The invention of the automobile, however, was the beginning of travel for pleasure by the average person.

As cities grew and the automobile became a family necessity, overcrowded downtowns were commonplace. It was no longer possible to move quickly in cities, bringing about the invention of the subway, streetcar, and bus. The world economy soon became dependent on the ability to transport goods, people, and ideas in record time. Of the ten largest industrial corporations in the world, seven are related to transportation. Two of the seven manufacture vehicles and the other five refine petroleum products for fueling the vehicles. It is estimated that 96 percent of the work force in the world depends on transportation to obtain their livelihoods.

Move It

Make a drawing of the progression of transportation followed in the poem.

Who just couldn't get into the groove.
He tried walking, of course,
Then he tamed him a horse.
But neither of these did behoove.

So he traveled the waters by boat.
Around the world he did float.
He could bring people things,
Oh he wished he had wings,
Because then he would have time to dote.

When he tired of riding a cart,
The man he became rather smart.
He invented the train,
Oh the miles he did gain.
Over prairies and fields he could dart.

There were those who traveled the sea.
Months and months on a ship they would be.
This was not very fast,
It would surely not last.
An airplane is what they did need.

When the flying machine was invented,
Quick travel could not be prevented.
Soon all could cavort,
With a passion of sorts.
And even the parents consented.

It's amazing the money that's made,
Because products can now be conveyed.
None of this would exist,
If man didn't insist,
On the fact that he just couldn't stay.

Ways to Deliver the Message

Use one of the following writing choices to tell the short history of your mode of transportation. Creativity is the key!

Cinquain

A cinquain is a poem designed in the shape of a diamond with a pattern:

noun
adjective, adjective
adverb, adverb, adverb
OR (verb, verb, verb)
metaphor
noun

bird
quick, light
flying, dipping, racing
messenger of song
high flier

Limerick

A limerick is a type of poem with five lines where the first, second, and fifth lines rhyme, and the third and fourth lines rhyme.

"Move It" example
is done in a limerick.

Tribute/Eulogy

Tributes and eulogies recognize someone or something for an accomplishment or a life of service. Tributes may be given to those living, while eulogies are done for the deceased.

"Passenger pigeons
are to be remembered
today for the faithful
service they performed. . ."

Interview with dialogue

Advertisement

Thank-you note

Ode

Newspaper article

Invitation

Diary entry

Recipe

Move It

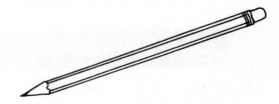

Directions: Read the "Move It By . . ." selection.

Look at the suggestions on the "Ways to Deliver the Message" sheet provided by the teacher. These are some creative ways to tell the class about the history of the mode of transportation about which you just read. Choose one of these delivery methods, or another that you may know, and create an original piece of writing that retells the history of the mode of transportation in your "Move It By . . ." selection.

Use the space below to write your final draft.

CHAPTER SIX

COMBINING THE FIVE THEMES OF GEOGRAPHY

Once students have an understanding of each of the Five Themes of Geography, they can apply them to any part of the social science curriculum. Whenever studying a country, the themes can be the focus of research or lesson planning for the teacher. As the introduction of the book explains, one reason geography education faded from curriculums was the lack of focused methods of teaching. These themes provide that focus and give structure to geography, encouraging the teaching about places without stereotypical, narrow ideas being translated to students.

In this final chapter, ideas are given about other ways the themes can be integrated within the social science class and in conjunction with other subjects. Teachers can use the five themes to organize lessons about countries and places. "Research Guidebook" is a lesson in this chapter that provides one idea for student country projects. Applying the five themes to design an imaginary world is another lesson. Finally, two possibilities for using the five themes with reading and language arts integration are shared.

There are unlimited areas of expansion using the themes described in this book. It is the author's hope that teachers will find ways to work in the five themes of geography as a curriculum organizational strategy. Once students become versed in the jargon of geography the world is an open book to be read over and over again from many perspectives.

Throw Me a Line

Objective: The student will analyze sentences to determine which of the five themes of geography is being revealed.

Preparation: Copy one "Throw Me a Line" student activity sheet for each student. Provide each student with a marker, a piece of construction paper, and a piece of masking tape. Side by side on the top of the chalkboard, write the five themes—location, place, human-environment interaction, movement, regions—leaving 18" between words.

Procedure: Pair students for this activity. Distribute an activity sheet to each pair, allowing them 10 minutes to complete it. When students are done, have them count off 1-20. On the construction paper, direct each student to write the sentence from the activity sheet that corresponds to the number they counted off. Those students who counted 11-20 write their own sentences on the construction paper. Have them write large enough words can be seen from a distance but small enough the whole sentence fits on one side of the paper.

As each student finishes writing, instruct him/her to tape the sentence on the board under the theme that he/she thinks is revealed in the sentence. When everyone has taped their sentences on the board, ask each student to find examples that do not agree with the answers he/she chose. If a discrepancy is found, the student should raise his/her hand. Select a student to come to the front and take down the sentence which is incorrectly placed. The student who put the sentence up then stands and defends why he/she thinks it was placed correctly. The student in front then states his/her argument. The class then votes on which defense they believe is the best and the sentence is placed under that theme.

All sentences do not have just one clear possibility. There is overlap in the themes and overlap in the sentences. Students will come to recognize this as the activity continues. It should be emphasized that as long as the answer can be defended it is correct, even if the class votes one defense as better than the other. There are often two or more "right" answers to things. Students correct their own papers as the class proceeds. Collect the papers at the end of class.

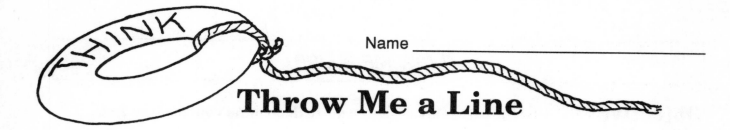

Name _____

Throw Me a Line

Directions: Each of the sentences below relates to one of the five themes of geography. Abbreviations for the five themes are given here. Identify which theme is revealed in each sentence by putting the abbreviation for that theme in the blank next to the sentence. Be able to defend why you chose each answer, as you may be called on to give a reason.

L = Location   P = Place   H-E-I = Human-Environment Interaction

M = Movement   R = Regions

1. _____ Kiwi fruit from New Zealand is on sale at the supermarket.

2. _____ Man has driven the black rhino to near extinction.

3. _____ In the bayous of Louisiana, many houses are built on stilts.

4. _____ Railroad networks in Europe make traveling easier for tourists.

5. _____ Deserts are not all hot and dry; Antarctica is a desert of sorts.

6. _____ Mauritania is southwest of Russia.

7. _____ The warmth of the southern states makes them attractive for retirement living.

8. _____ Islam is the major religion in the MidEast.

9. _____ Sheep are raised in Iceland for the wool used in Icelandic sweaters.

10. _____ The mountain passes of the Rockies are treacherous in winter and even a bit scary in summer.

Write one sentence of your own that relates to one of the five themes:
(If working in pairs, each student writes his/her own sentence here.)

Design a World

One final product for the five themes unit is for students to design a country, from a fictitious world, using the five themes. Included in this lesson plan is an example of a fictitious world map the teacher may use. He/She may design a map or have students design one. Ideas for project requirements are shared. The procedure for this lesson is in narrative form.

This is an alternative assessment that will genuinely evaluate a student's ability to apply the themes. The overall project will take three weeks if done in entirety. However, the author suggests that pieces be done at appropriate times in a five themes unit. For example, each Friday students would work on a piece of this project, while Monday through Thursday developmental lessons on the themes will be conducted. When the five themes unit is complete, the final pieces of this project would be put in place. Students would then be able to demonstrate their understanding of the five themes, not as separate themes, but as a wholistic way of viewing geography.

Objective: Students will apply knowledge and understanding of the five themes of geography to design a country in a fictitious world.

Preparation: Preparation will depend on which ideas the teacher chooses to employ for this project. Ideas described in the procedure will include preparation needs.

Procedure:

Developmental Activities: Students will be shown the "Design a World" map. In pairs, students are assigned one of the spaces and will create a country within its boundaries.

Location: A discussion about the equator and hemispheres will be conducted by the teacher.

Place: Many of a country's characteristics are determined by climate and physical features. Therefore, the project will begin with a lesson on "What Causes Climate" to facilitate students in designing their countries' physical and human characteristics.

Students will design topography and determine climate restrictions as a first step in designing the country. Then, with topography and climate as givens, students will place cities and choose natural resources that are appropriate to their country's design. They will draw maps showing topography, cities, and climate. (See requirements below for more explanation.)

Human-Environment Interaction: With resources now as a given, an original product that can be produced in the country will be designed. Students will develop a marketing plan for this product. Up to this point, only physical geography has been considered.

Place: The human factors can be examined in these ways. Students can identify on a "Fact Sheet" some of the human features that they want to exist. By creating a "Culture Collage," students can show humans at work and play. Once this collage is done, have students look at the pictures carefully. What kinds of products are in the pictures they have drawn or chosen? Are homes made of wood? Are people wearing leather? Is anyone driving a car? What natural resources, chosen by the students, do they have in their country to support these items? All students will find products that their countries are not able to produce due to climate and land form restrictions. This means they will need to import. "Resource Roundup" is an activity that demonstrates that interdependence will be needed even in this fictitious world.

For students to further apply the **Human-Environment Interaction** theme, the teacher may want to incorporate a research project. This will add time to the project. One idea is for this to be going on simultaneously in language arts class, making this an interdisciplinary project. The teacher would ask students to brainstorm as many ways as possible in which people interact with the environment. Many issues, from waste disposal, to endangered species, to natural-disaster planning (students love to have volcanoes, for instance, in their topography), to recreational opportunities will arise in the discussion. Students could choose or be assigned one of the issues or topics to research. They could research it in the interest of their fictitious country's government and make a plan to deal with it in a positive way. If this project is too time consuming, the theme could be developed by having students build a model of a practical home for their region or design a traditional clothing outfit that is suitable for the climate and culture.

Regions, as a theme, is a way for students to compare and contrast places. Teachers could do a lesson where similarities and differences between the fictitious countries are highlighted. Ask students to find another country created by peers that has five characteristics similar to theirs. Ask students to group themselves according to regions. For example, the teacher may say, "Any students whose country has a tropical climate stand near the window." "Any students whose country has a major crop-producing region sit on the floor." This might be a good activity to do before "Resource Roundup" so that students have an idea about the nature of the other countries that have been designed. One final idea for regions is to have students identify their own regional characteristics or those of another country in a written description of the country. This would be an evaluation piece for the teacher in determining student understanding.

Along the way, the "Fact Sheet" will be completed.

The final portion of this project is the creation of a three-dimensional topographical, political map by each student pair. A time and resources management plan of how to implement this activity is included in this lesson to encourage teachers to try this portion of the project. It is the part that students seem to like best.

Culminating Activities: When all the pieces are in place, students should have the opportunity to display their hard work as a finished product. A "Design a World Fair" is one possibility. Have students set up a display booth of all the pieces they worked on for this project. They may want to prepare other promotional items as well, such as travel brochures, ethnic foods, musical recordings, and others. Set up a schedule where half the students oversee their booths while the other half travel around looking at the displays. Switch so that the other half can enjoy the festivities. Invite parents and other classes. This is an authentic assessment that students will remember with pride.

Overview of the Project: Student pairs should have a folder in which to
organize materials and paperwork. Ultimately, students may end with the following items as part of the project whole.

THREE HAND-DRAWN MAPS

> **Topographical**– Students must put ten land forms in their country. (See "Natural Resource Crop List" of definitions.)

> **Political**–Students must identify five cities with locations and names. Reasoning behind placing these cities may be asked for by the teacher.

> **Climate**–Students will show with colors and a key how the climate in their country is effected by latitude, location, and land forms. Justification for climate changes must be provided in an explanation to the teacher.

FACT SHEET DESCRIBING THE COUNTRY–Adapt an appropriate fact sheet from the data collection device entitled "Fairy Tale Frolics."

ORIGINAL PRODUCT DESIGN–Students create a product that the country could produce with the natural resources available to them. Natural resources are chosen from a list before this assignment is given. The fact sheet would list resources chosen by students.

CULTURE COLLAGE–drawings and magazine cutouts, arranged on a poster or such, showing the people and their homes, clothing, and life style.

RESOURCE ROUNDUP–a document that shows students have communicated about imports and exports with other students

THREE-DIMENSIONAL MAP–includes 10 topographical features, 5 cities/towns, 5 representative items of products grown/mined/produced, and a key

Possibly:

HUMAN-ENVIRONMENT INTERACTION PORTION–research paper or other

REGIONS PORTION–written assignment or other

THREE-DIMENSIONAL MAP MANAGEMENT PLAN—Time, Resources, and Procedure

Who   Student pairs work together on their country.
What   Making salt and flour dough maps.
Where   In the classroom
When   3 periods
Why   Culminating project for "Design a World."
How Much   45 maps/$40.00/two 25-lb. bags of flour and a case of salt.

Cardboard Building Surface—First, go to an appliance store and get some big boxes. Cut them into cardboard pieces about 2' x 2½' with a utility knife. Make enough so that you have one piece for each country in the fictitious world. Trace one country's outline onto each piece of cardboard using an opaque projector or overhead projector.

Dough—Get a few buckets in which to mix the dough. Pour half a bag of flour into the bucket and add some water, enough so that the dough is pliable but not sticky. Mix with your hands. Add four or five containers of salt and mix. The dough should be a bit gritty, not too dry or too wet. It is a trial-and-error mixing job but hard to ruin; almost any mixture will work.

Set Up—Put newspapers on tables in your room. Arrange for no more than three pairs of students per table. Lay the cardboard pieces on the tables and let students find their country outline. Have them get a few handfuls of dough and plop them into the middle of their outline. Then they press the dough out toward the edges and shape it to fit their outline. Too thin will crack easily, but too thick will never dry. About ½" thick works well.

Land Forms—Have students build up the mountains, hills, and plateaus by pushing existing dough into ridges. If they try to make the mountains separately and then stick them on, they will fall off when it dries. Carve out the rivers, lakes, and canyons. They may add texture to the deserts and plains. Plastic utensils are good tools to use. It helps if students pat flour on their hands if the dough is sticky.

Allow one 45-minute period for this part of the project. Let them dry for two or three days.

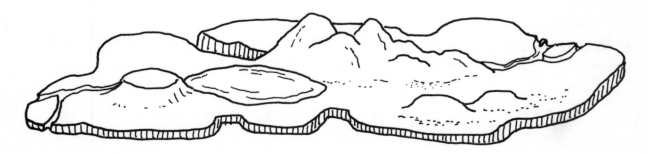

Painting–Consider putting little butter tubs of each color on each table so students will not need to carry paint from table to table. This avoids spills. Set up a designated color key for painting the land forms or let students design a key of their own.

Use one class period for painting! Let them dry overnight.

Labeling–Give each pair of students five white stickers–small labels–on which to write the names of their cities and towns. They should place them where they have designated cities on the original political map they designed. They may also want to label land forms if they have come up with names for them.

Resources–The day before labeling is to take place, assign students to bring five items that represent products in their country. They will glue them on wherever appropriate. For example, they might glue a few pieces of popcorn on one of the plains because they grow corn there and glue green sequins on the mountains because they mine emeralds there.

Key–Students create a key that is attached to their cardboard. The key shows what land forms the colors represent and what resources the items represent.

Title–Have them design a title on white construction paper that has the name of the country and its flag on it. Glue this to the cardboard, also.

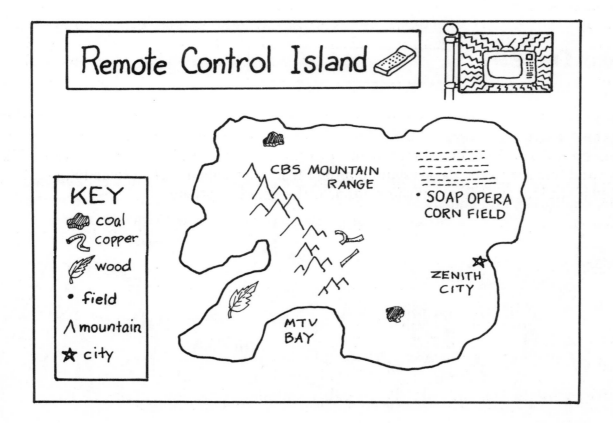

Original Product Design Assignment

Think of a product that you could make in your country using the natural resources that you have chosen. The product must be one that can be sold to the general public. For example: cereal, surfboards, a video game, etc.

Think of an original name for the product.

Develop an advertising campaign for the product. It must include two of the following things:

- poster advertising the product
- script of a television commercial for the product that you will eventually perform
- prototype of the product—either actual size or a model of a different size

> Assignment Requirements:

* Must be an original name, not one that already exists.
* Must do two of the above choices.
* Must be neat and colorful.
* Must be turned in on time.

Due Date:

Culture Collage

Using your own artist abilities and/or magazine cutouts, illustrate in a collage the life style, traditions, and culture of the people in your country. Plan your collage so that it is neat and touches on a variety of things. Some possible ideas to include are:

Design a World

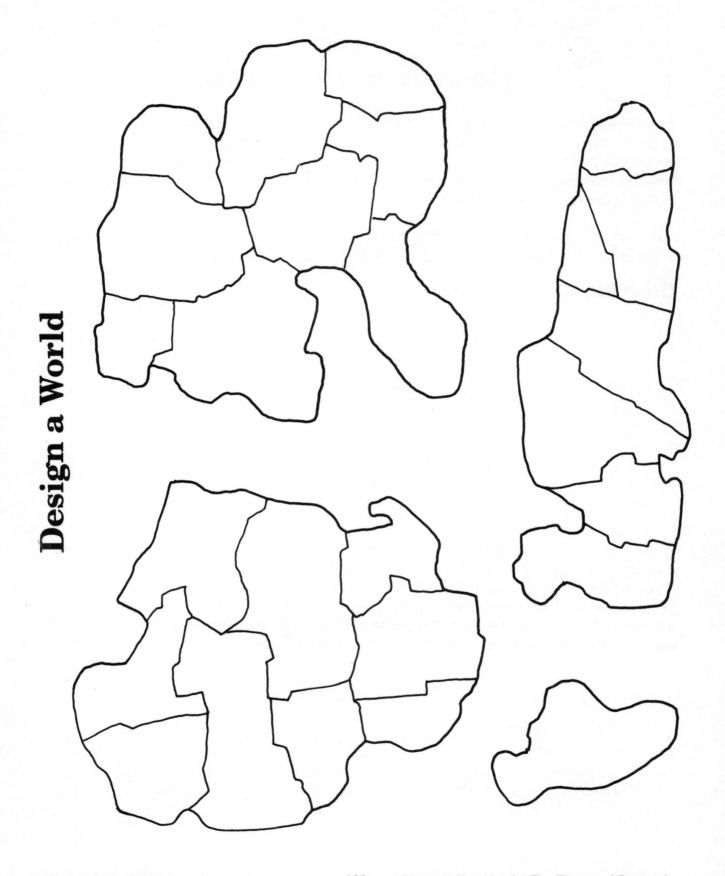

109

Name _____

Resource Roundup

Directions: With your partner, look carefully at the pictures you have drawn or selected in your culture collage. Notice the clothing people are wearing. Notice the materials needed to build the homes and other structures. Notice the food being eaten and the vehicles being operated. Below, list as many of the materials as you can that are used to build, make, or provide these products to your people.

For example: If someone is wearing jeans, you would list *cotton* as a material needed to make jeans. If someone is wearing a diamond ring, you would list *gold* and *diamonds*.

List of Materials/Resources:

When you are done with the list, compare it to the list of natural resources that your country is set up to provide. If you grow *cotton* you can make jeans in your country. But if you do not mine *gold* and *diamonds*, you will need to import those things for your people to have them available. Anything on the list that is not found in your country according to your original plan should be put in one of the boxes found on the next page. There are nine boxes; choose nine things from your list.

In each box put one resource material that you will have to import.

When the teacher directs you, mingle with other students in the room, trying to find a country designed by your peers that can export each material to your country. Fill in the name of the exporting countries in the spaces provided.

exporter:	exporter:	exporter:
exporter:	exporter:	exporter:
exporter:	exporter:	exporter:

Challenge: If some of the materials are not produced in any of the countries designed by your classmates, you may try this challenge. You can look up those materials to determine the kind of land forms/climate needed to produce them. If you have the appropriate situation in your country, then you may add those products to your resource list. If you do not, you must find a country that does have the correct conditions to produce that material. Convince the designers of that country to add the material to their resource list so that you may import from them.

What Causes Climate?   Teacher Resource Page

I. Latitude Affects Climate

1. **Low latitude zone**:   hot/warm year round
                                  Equator to 30°N/S
2. **Middle latitude zone**: cool/cold winters, hot/warm summers
                                  30°N/S to 60°N/S
3. **High latitude zone**:   cool/cold year round
                                  60° N/S to Poles

II. Elevation Affects Climate

1. The higher above sea level a place is, the cooler its climate.
2. The closer to sea level a place is, the warmer its climate.
3. For every 1,000 feet above sea level, the temperature changes approximately 3.5° F.

III. Large Bodies of Water Affect Climate

1. In the summer, water warms more slowly than land. The cool breezes off the water cause the summer climate to be cooler near the coast than it is inland.
2. In the winter, water cools more slowly than land. The warm breezes off the water cause the winter climate near the coast to be milder than it is inland. This leads to the conclusion: Places near the ocean or large lakes are not as hot in the summer or cold in the winter as places with the same elevation and latitude that are not near the water.

IV. Other Factors Affect Climate

1. **Moisture** in the air, from humidity to precipitation, is largely determined by amounts of vegetation and proximity to bodies of water.
2. **Wind** from polar or tropical regions can carry such varying temperatures that normal climate is disrupted.
3. **Ocean currents**, warm or cold, tend to make the land near to where they travel warmer or colder than expected at certain times.

Natural Resource/Crop List   Teacher Resource Page

Students can select appropriate products from the list below by determining which items coordinate with the land forms they have planned into their countries.

Products	Geographic Area	Climate
corn	plains	temperate
wheat	plains	temperate
potato	mountains/fields	temperate
beans	fields	temperate
cotton	fields/hills	temperate
sugar beets	fields/plains	temperate
coal	various	temperate
sheep	plains/hills	temperate
trees	various	various
gravel	valleys/rivers/seashore	various
uranium	mountains/near lakes	various
iron ore	various	various
silver	various	various
natural gas	rocky areas/off shore	various
gold	mountains/streams	various
fish	lakes/oceans	various
oil	deserts/plains/off shore	various
emeralds	mountains	various
rice	flooded, swampy plains wetlands	tropical
coffee	mountains	tropical
bananas	lowlands/hills	tropical
citrus fruits	lowlands	tropical
sugar cane	fields/plains	tropical
rubies	mountains/valleys	tropical
diamonds	gravel stream beds volcanic areas	tropical
cattle	plains/hills	temperate/tropical

If students want to produce an item not on this list, they will need to research its appropriate location of occurrence.

The Five Themes and Fairy Tale Frolics

Fairy tales are, of course, make-believe. Therefore, they do not take place anywhere in the real world. It is interesting, however, when looking at legends, myths, and tales from cultures all over the world, that similarities in stories appear. The same lessons are expressed by people from many different places and times in history. The differences are in the settings, the dress, the food, and the life styles of the characters. Cultures make their stories agree with their familiar surroundings and ways of life so that the young people they are intended for can relate to the tales. This strategy of recognizable settings will hopefully drive the message home more readily, teaching lessons about culture, manners, and values.

The five themes of geography provide a structure for successful frolicking with fairy tales. Students will take well-known stories and customize them into tales with a well-defined setting, relating not only the message of the tale but geographic/cultural awareness.

Objective: Students will apply their knowledge of the five themes of geography to create "new" fairy tales.

Preparation: There are a few options from which to choose when doing this activity. Once again, ideas are based on a 20-student classroom. The teacher may select the tales to modify and assign them to students or have them randomly choose titles from a hat. Suggestions for tales that seem to fit well with this activity are given below. Each student may get a different tale, requiring 20 tales; students can be paired for an assigned tale, making 10 different tales; or the teacher can select five tales and have two pairs working on the same tale.

Another option is to have students select their own tales from fairy tale anthologies that the teacher would provide. This second option would give students more choice but would be time consuming, as students would need to read many tales before selecting one. Choose one of these options and proceed. This book focuses on pairing students and providing five tales.

Suggestions: "The Real Princess" (The Princess and the Pea), "Briar Rose" (Sleeping Beauty), "Little Red Riding Hood," "Rumpelstiltskin," "Rapunzel"

Select five tales; copy them from a book or retype them. Make four copies of each tale. Pair students and distribute the tales randomly, giving partners the same tale. There will be two pairs working on "Cinderella," two working on "Rapunzel," etc. It is surprising how many different ways a story can be told, so there is no reason to be worried about redundancy.

Procedure: Instruct the pairs to read the story through once. Give each pair a "Fairy Tale Frolics" sheet to complete by researching a country of their choice or the teacher's selection. Once the sheet is complete, the pair works to insert the details from the sheet into the story.

Give each pair a piece of poster-sized paper and a "Fairy Tale Frolics Poster Instructions" sheet. Following the directions, pairs develop a poster of their tale as a finished product. Rewriting is the first step. The goal is to leave the story intact as much as possible, taking out only the things that are in disagreement with the location chosen by the students. As an option, the teacher might encourage students to add humorous details or modernize the story. The students can white out, use arrow inserts, or make notes. When the story is adjusted sufficiently, the students rewrite it in final draft form. They then design a poster as the directions explain.

Have students read their stories aloud to the class and share their posters. The audience can help with the evaluation of the project, using the peer evaluation form provided. If distributed when the project is assigned, the peer evaluation form will help students to focus on quality.

The class will learn about the human and physical geography of different places in the world just by listening to each others' stories. The teacher will know if the projects meet this goal by reading the peer evaluations.

Display the posters under the heading "The Five Themes of Geography and Fairy Tale Frolics."

Fairy Tale Frolics

Directions: Choose a country in the world that you would like to know more about or work with the country assigned to you by the teacher. Answer the questions below by researching the country, using two sources of information. Your partner should use one source and you should use another. Later you will compare and combine the information you have both found.

LOCATION

Name of country: _____

Name, longitude/latitude of capital city: _____

Distance in miles and cardinal direction(s) traveled to get to the country from your hometown: _____

PLACE

(Choose a season in which to set the tale.)

Climate: _____

Prominent physical features (proper names) in the country: _____

_____

_____

Prominent race of people who live in the country: _____

Animals and plants found in the country: _____

_____

_____

Customs, religions, occupations, language, clothing styles, and holidays.

_____

_____

_____

(use another sheet if needed)

HUMAN-ENVIRONMENT INTERACTION

Prominent housing style in the country and why this type of house is practical:

_____

_____

Crops/livestock raised, resources mined and/or harvested: _____

_____

Environmental problems/solutions that exist in the country:_____

_____

_____

Type of clothing worn in the country during
the season chosen: _____

_____

MOVEMENT

Popular modes of transportation in the country: _____

_____

Exports: _____

Imports: _____

Popular modes of communication in the country: _____

_____

Regions

(The theme of regions is a review of all the other themes, giving us a way to compare
and contrast places around the world. By filling in the information below, you will have
a quick reference of the most prominent characteristics of the country you are
researching.)

Language(s): _____

Government: _____

Climate: _____

Religion: _____

Physical features: _____

_____

Ways in which the country is similar to your own country:_____

_____

_____

_____

Fairy Tale Frolics
Poster Instructions

Partners:

1. Research a country by completing the "Fairy Tale Frolics" sheet.

Rewrite the Fairy Tale

Goal: To retell the story as if it takes place in the country you researched. You must be sure that the main idea or message of the story remains intact.

2. Together, read through the story, deleting any details that do not agree with the information you found out about the country you researched. Replace those details with things that are consistent with the culture of the country researched. For example, if in the country researched the people live in tents and in the fairy tale there is a castle, this must be changed. The castle might become a large tent.

3. Go back through the information sheet and make a mark next to any detail you have included in the story so far.

4. Select more items of information from your research to include in the story. Work the information in creatively throughout the tale. You may change as much as you want, as long as it does not change the main idea of the story. One thing to consider is the name of the main character, should it be changed to a name that seems more appropriate for the country researched?

5. Once all the changes have been made and agreed upon, write a final draft on school paper or word processor. If it is more than one side of one piece of paper, go on to a new sheet instead of turning the paper over.

Continue the project by following the directions on the next page.

Design a Fairy Tale Frolics Poster

Goal: To show, on a poster, how the five themes of geography have been worked into the fairy tale.

6. Using the design shown here (or another idea, if approved by the teacher), develop a poster with drawings, pictures from magazines, or cartoons.

Location	Place
Written story here / **Human Environment** / **Interaction** / **Written story here**	
Movement	Regions

Pay attention to neatness, use of color, size of drawings (large enough to see from a short distance), and due date requirements. Partners should share the work equally.

Project Goal: Through a fairy tale and poster, communicate the human and physical geography of a foreign country.

Peer Evaluation

Name of Evaluator _____

Name of Peers Being Evaluated _____

_____

Project Goal: Through a fairy tale and poster, communicate the human and physical geography of a foreign country.

This evaluation asks questions about the project done by your peers. If you can answer these questions, the students that you are evaluating have done a good job in reaching the goal of the project. Complete both sides of this form.

1. What country is the setting of the tale?

2. Name three things that describe the way people live in the country that is the setting.

   _____

   _____

   _____

3. Look at the pictures on the poster. For each picture, describe why you think they chose that picture to represent the geographic theme.

Location:

Place:

Human-Environment Interaction:

Movement:

Regions:

Name _____

Answer these questions and give point values that you believe are fair.

1. What is one thing you really liked about the story and poster you are evaluating?

2. There are always ways to improve our work. What is one thing that would make the project you are evaluating even better?

3. Along with content, projects are also assessed for other factors. Give the project you are evaluating points for the following things according to this scale:

> 5 = best it could possibly be   4 = very good
> 3 = meets the requirement   2 = needs much improvement
> 1 = poor

neatness

overall, looks organized and put together with thought   _____

written piece is in final draft form   _____

drawings/pictures are neatly done and eyecatching   _____

project is complete, all pieces are done with equal quality   _____

deadline

project is done and turned in on time   _____

total   _____

This form will be given to the students who did the project. The teacher will use the information gathered here to assess if the project meets the goals. One quarter of the grade (25 pts.) will be based on the points given above. An average of the peer evaluator's score and the teacher's score may be taken. Students are encouraged to discuss with their peers any questions or disagreements about ratings and responses. The teacher may choose to give improvement opportunities based on suggestions.

Other Ideas:

Incorporating the Five Themes of Geography into the Curriculum

When students do a writing project about personal experience, have them highlight or comment on ways the five themes are revealed in the writing.

Design a special writing project that has students using the five themes as a factor of development. One idea is:

Students will produce a written journal that simulates a journal written by them as they are deserted on an island, waiting to be rescued. Each day in class, students are given a new obstacle or dilemma to deal with. They express their solutions in the journal. The problems each day will relate to the five themes. For example one day the teacher may say, "Your island has fruit trees growing near your campsite, a site chosen because from it you can easily spot passing ships. Since it has not rained for the entire two weeks you've been here, the trees need water. There is a river about one mile away but you have no bucket. How will you get water to the trees to ensure a fruit supply? Remember, you do not know how long you will be trapped on the island." This dilemma deals with Human-Environment Interaction and Place themes.

When students research a country for a social science project, design the project outcomes to focus on the five themes. Ideas from the lesson entitled "Fairy Tale Frolics" may be helpful in implementing this idea.

As students read trade books for book reports, have them share how the themes are revealed to the reader in the setting. When the story is set in a foreign country, culture is usually a rich part of the setting and can easily be recognized as the theme of place. Make it extra credit for students who share these discoveries.

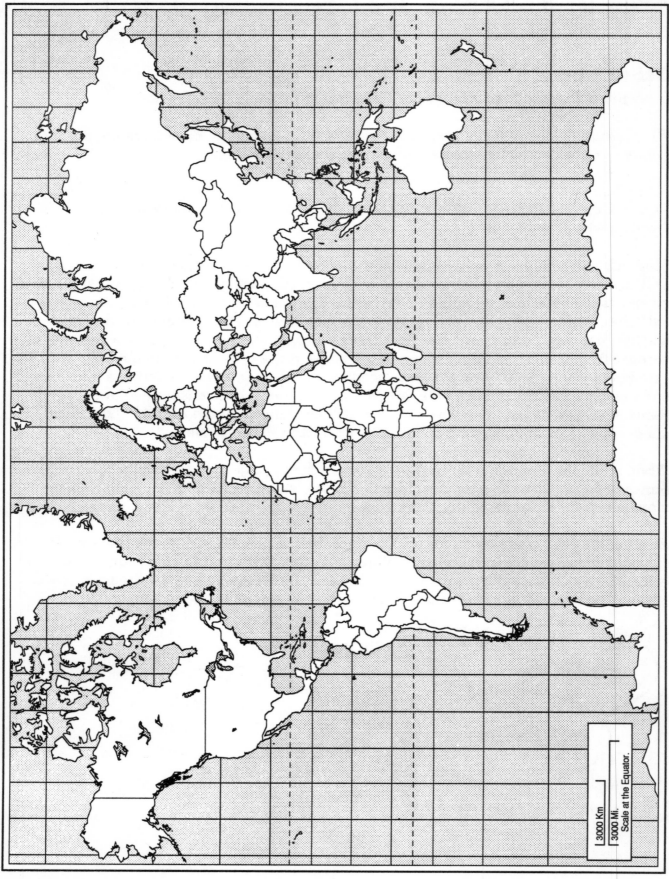

World Map

3000 Km
3000 Mi.
Scale at the Equator.